# THE
# Meanderings
## OF MY
# Muddled
# Mind

Craig Wood

**WESTBOW**
PRESS®
A DIVISION OF THOMAS NELSON
& ZONDERVAN

WestBow Press books may be ordered through booksellers or by contacting:

WestBow Press
A Division of Thomas Nelson & Zondervan
1663 Liberty Drive
Bloomington, IN 47403
www.westbowpress.com
844-714-3454

Scripture quotations are from the Revised Standard Version of the
Bible, copyright © 1946, 1952, and 1971 the Division of Christian
Education of the National Council of the Churches of Christ in the
United States of America. Used by permission. All rights reserved.

ISBN: 978-1-6642-1700-3 (sc)
ISBN: 978-1-6642-1702-7 (hc)
ISBN: 978-1-6642-1701-0 (e)

Library of Congress Control Number: 2020925397

Print information available on the last page.

WestBow Press rev. date: 1/13/2021

At present we see indistinctly, as in a mirror, but then face to face. At present I know partially; then I shall know fully, as I am fully known.
—Paul, 1 Corinthians 13:12

# preface

This book is a compilation of a few years' worth of monthly columns written for a church newsletter. Many of the members of that church encouraged me to have the columns published, which I have decided to do now that I have been retired for a while. As you will see, events that happen to all of us every day sometimes start my mind meandering about what we know and don't know about God and what we can learn from the message of Jesus.

I often find these everyday events humorous; so hopefully you can be entertained as well as inspired to do some thinking of your own regarding these topics. The title of the book is based on St. Paul's idea that our vision is muddled, but somehow we need to keep seeking. Our knowledge will always be incomplete; but it never hurts to seek the kingdom of Heaven.

Some people have found it useful to consider these topics in small group discussions, sharing ideas with each other; and there are questions at the end of each chapter to stimulate such discussions. Others have enjoyed reading the chapters alone and just allowing their minds to meander all on their own.

# acknowledgments

I am thankful to the many members of the Heartland Vineyard Church in Cedar Falls, Iowa, who encouraged me to have *The Meanderings of My Muddled Mind* published. In addition, I am thankful to the senior pastor of that church, Dan Paxton, for asking me to write a column for the monthly newsletter. Most of this book consists of those columns. I am appreciative of my wife's cousin, Jan Edwards, whose editing was so helpful, and of my wife, Candy, who puts up with my meanderings daily.

# chapter one

# If I Knew Then What I Know Now

I was brushing my teeth the other day and realized that about half of my teeth are made of metal. That is because when I was young, I didn't brush my teeth. So half of my real teeth have been replaced with metal crowns. I've got so much metal in my teeth that when I go for my checkups, they don't check for cavities; they check for rust.

But I was thinking about when I was a kid, and I would trick my mom into thinking I had brushed my teeth by rubbing my front teeth with my washcloth. When she checked my teeth, she just said, "Smile"; she never really checked my back teeth. I don't really know what I had against brushing my teeth. Maybe it was that, in a family with four kids and two adults sharing one bathroom, the toothpaste lid was often left off the tube, and the first quarter inch was hard like a rock. That grossed me out.

My parents both had false teeth by the time they were thirty. Dad claimed it was because of the lousy water he had to drink overseas during World War II. Mom just said she had soft teeth. But I remember they always said, "If you don't brush your teeth, you'll end up needing false teeth like us." I looked at them and thought to myself, "Those look pretty good to me." I guess I just didn't believe that brushing your teeth was a big deal. Now the only teeth I have left without metal are the front ones that I rubbed with a washcloth every day.

These days, they don't hand out false teeth as they used to. They are more likely to do a root canal and put a metal cap on what's left of the tooth. Or if it's really bad they might pull the tooth and insert a dental implant, which is basically screwing in a new tooth. So instead of just torturing you once, pulling all of your teeth at once, and getting it over with, you might have to go in several times to get all your teeth taken care of. If you're a dentist, I'm sorry, but I hate going to the dentist. I had one once who said, "Do you want laughing gas, Novocain, or head phones with music?" I said, "I want everything you've got. In fact, if you want to put me to sleep and wake me when it's over, that would be okay too." And that was just for the checkup.

Anyway, I was remembering the bad brushing habits I had as a kid, and I said to myself, "I wish I knew then what I know now." How often do you say that to yourself? I say it quite a bit actually. Somebody once said, "Youth is wasted on the young." I'm pretty sure that if I had it to do over again, I would do quite a few things differently. For one thing, I'd do a better job of brushing my teeth. Yup, I sure wish I knew then what I know now.

Craig Wood

But then my mind started meandering. I was thinking that I'm really kind of a child in God's eyes. There are a lot of things God knows that I don't know. I hope I don't grow up spiritually and someday say, "I wish I could do it all over again. I wish I knew then what I know now." I wonder if I could figure out what mistakes I'm making now. I'd kind of like to be able to know now what I will say I wish I knew when I become a spiritual adult.

So I started going through the Bible to see what it said about growing up spiritually and what it means for us now. Probably the best-known passage about growing up is the part in the "love chapter"—1 Corinthians 13:9–13. In there, it says, "For now we know partially and we prophesy partially, but when the perfect comes, the partial will pass away. When I was a child, I used to talk as a child, think as a child, reason as a child; when I became a man, I put aside childish things. At present we see indistinctly as in a mirror, but then face to face. At present I know partially; then I shall know fully, as I am fully known. So faith, hope, love remain, these three; but the greatest of these is love."

In the days when that was written, "mirrors" were not the perfect reflection that we have today. They were more like seeing your reflection in a window or pool of water. In other words, the reflection was quite a bit different from reality. So Paul was saying that at present, we see a distorted version of reality; so the best thing to do is love others.

What I get from all of that is that I can brush my teeth, wash my face, comb my hair, and dress up all I want, but if I don't love people, I'm still going to fall short of what God wants me to be. The good news is that God loves me anyway.

Hmm …

—If you had your life to live over, what are some things you might do differently?

—How are you different now from when you first became a Christian?

—How does one "grow" spiritually?

—What do you consider to be indications of spiritual maturity?

# chapter two

## Soup and Salt

I recently heard a sermon about soup. So lately my mind has been meandering about the topic of soup ingredients. Specifically, I've been thinking about ingredients for vegetable soup. The pastor said we are to love the whole church including all the denominations, and he compared all of the churches as a whole to a big pot of soup. He fancied himself to be a carrot. The carrot, you know, is that long slim vegetable, broad at the shoulders and narrow at the hip. Far be it from me to mess with the pastor's fantasy. My wife said I was probably a rutabaga. I don't even know whether to be offended, because I don't know what a rutabaga looks like.

I started to think about all of the various "soup ingredients" I have been involved in. Let's see, I've been a member of the Church of Christ, a Baptist, a Nazarene, a Methodist, a Presbyterian, and a member of the Vineyard Christian Fellowship. When I was stationed at the US Military Academy in West Point, New York, we attended fairly regularly a folk mass conducted at a Roman

Catholic monastery just across the Hudson River. That was our first exposure to contemporary Christian music in worship. All of these experiences had something to offer the "soup" of my Christian journey.

The Baptists loved to sing. They would sing only a couple of verses of each hymn so they could work in more hymns. They used to have members of the congregation shout out requests. As a kid, I always requested "Onward Christian Soldiers." probably because it's the coolest hymn there is for a drummer if you can't do contemporary Christian music.

The Nazarenes have a lot of audience participation during the sermon. They're always shouting "Amen" or "That's Right" or "Praise the Lord." They could get more worked up during a sermon than during the singing.

The Methodists were big into fellowship. We had more pot luck dinners in the one year we were Methodists than in several years of other churches. And hardly anybody went straight home after the service; they gathered in the "fellowship hall" for coffee and gab.

The Presbyterians were notable because of their work in social action. Both of the Presbyterian churches we belonged to were very much into feeding the hungry, clothing the naked, visiting the imprisoned, and tending to the sick.

The Vineyard Christian Fellowship has a powerful worship experience through contemporary Christian music and a strong outreach program.

Thus, singing, getting excited hearing the Word of God, socializing with fellow Christians, helping others, and playing drums in a Christian worship band all became the vegetables in my personal Christian soup. But all these churches brought something similar to the larger pot of soup that makes up the world. After thinking about that for a while, I remembered what Jesus said of Christians in the world. He said we are the salt of the earth. We are the salt in the soup. In addition to being a flavoring agent, salt is an essential nutrient for humans, like water; we couldn't live without it.

In the old days before refrigeration, salt was also a major preservative, used to keep meat from spoiling. Salt, in fact, is a form of the word *salvation*. So, it ought to be a common goal of the church to keep humanity from spoiling—to be the essential ingredient that makes humans tasteful or desirable. Whew! That's a pretty heavy responsibility!

Hmm …

—How are we Christians doing at being the "salt of the earth" do you think? How could we do better?

—How do you interact with people who have chosen a different denomination, or no church at all?

—As what soup ingredient would you see yourself?

chapter three

# chapter three

---

# Lost and Found

---

You'd think that by the time you got to be my age, you'd know just about everything. But I have to confess that there are quite a few things I still find puzzling. One of these things is why they call the Lost and Found box the Lost *and Found* box. If I lost something, and I don't know it's in that box, it's still lost until I find it. Am I right? Okay, some people are going to say that somebody else found it and put it in the box; therefore, it has been lost *and* found. But I still say that until the owner finds it, it is just plain lost. So I say the box ought to be called the Box of the Lost.

I guess it depends on how you define "lost."

One time we were in a big city on vacation, and I took the wrong exit off the main interstate highway. The exit wound around (meandered, you might say) down to a one-way street, and it was nighttime, so I had a hard time trying to figure out how to get back on the interstate. In fact, before long we couldn't even see the interstate any more. My wife said, "Okay, Craig, just admit it: you're lost." Looking at the street signs, I said, "I'm not lost, I know exactly where I am. I'm at the corner of Thirty-Second Street and Jackson." She replied, "Yes, but you don't know how to get where you're going." It was another one of those things on how you define "lost."

Some evangelistic types have been known to start their work by asking the question "Have you found Jesus?" When my mother-in-law was alive, she used to travel quite a bit visiting her son who was stationed overseas, after which she would return and stay with us a while. We always enjoyed the tales of her travels. She had been a Sunday school teacher for some fifty years, so she kind of knew about Jesus. One time she told us about one of the "Jesus people," who were these young evangelists that used to hang out at airports more than they do now it seems. She said that one of them came up to her and asked her if she had found Jesus. Her reply was, "Young man, I didn't know He was lost."

They had a good laugh, and she testified about how God had worked in her life, and they parted friends.

The point of her reply was that we don't find Jesus, because Jesus is not lost. *We* are lost. Jesus finds us. In fact, that is one of the main reasons Jesus was born. Jesus says in Luke 19:10 that "the Son of Man has come to seek and save the lost." Jesus knew who He was, knew where He was from, and knew where He was going. He definitely was not lost no matter how you define it.

Sometimes we Christians make the mistake of taking pride in our salvation, as if it is a result of something we did. Sometimes it seems as if instead of singing "Amazing grace/how sweet the sound/I once was lost/but now I'm found," we want to sing,

"Amazing grace/how sweet the sound/I once was naughty, but now I'm nice." That doesn't even rhyme.

Anyway, I think the definition of being lost is being separated from the owner. In fact, some have said that the definition of "living in sin" is living separated from God. We need to remember that we were all in the Box of the Lost once, and we are really no better than those who are still in it. We need to pray that God will find all of His lost sheep. We can certainly be grateful that God found us. That is truly amazing.

Hmm …

—Describe how it feels to you to be found by God. Did you feel lost before you were found?

—If you are still feeling lost, or separated from God, do you think there is anything you can do to help become found?

—Do you know where you are religiously? Do you know where you want to go?

—If you and your parents went to church, and you have always been a Christian, how does this Lost and Found concept work for you? Is it possible that you were never lost?

*chapter four*

# Obeying the Rules

Here's an old brainteaser: If a tree falls in the forest, but there is nobody there to hear it, is there a sound? People have come to fisticuffs debating the answer to that question. If you get that one settled, here's another one: If a man makes a decision, but there is no woman around to hear it, is he still wrong?

I was thinking about that the other morning when my wife had spent the previous night away from home, and I was deciding whether to make the bed. I was likely to be in bed again that night before she got home; so, she'd never know whether I made the bed. My wife has a thing about making the bed. She makes the bed if she has a cast on her arm, or if she's on crutches, or, well, no matter what.

I, on the other hand, think it's okay to not make the bed if nobody is going to see it. If I make the bed, then I just have to unmake it when I get in it that night. And frankly, I don't think God cares. I'd like to know where it says in the Bible that people have to make their beds. But I had a dilemma. She might not know whether I made the bed, but she might ask me. Then I'd have to confess that I had not.

Living by checking the rule book all the time is really nerve-racking. Should I do this? Should I do that? What's right? What's wrong? Sometimes it even seems that being a Christian is all about following rules, obeying the law. The first five books of the Bible are even called "The Law." There we find the Ten Commandments (and about six hundred other commandments as well). There's even a law (Leviticus 11:20–23) that says you can eat grasshoppers and locusts but no other winged insects that crawl on all fours. Not that I'd want to eat any of those insects, mind you, permitted or not. Some laws are easy for me to obey.

Our church has encouraged the development of discussion groups that meet in family homes and discuss the Bible or books, and in our group, we're discussing the book *What's So Amazing About Grace*, by Philip Yancey, and talking about God's grace. The world's major religions nearly all have laws that, if people obeyed them, would keep the world in pretty good shape. One of the unique features of our Christian faith is the concept of grace. To me, the concept of grace is best defined by the picture in Luke 15:20 of the prodigal son's father running—not walking but running—to welcome home his sinful son. The son did not even have to ask for forgiveness; the father forgave him first. As John 1:17 says, "For while the Law was given through Moses, the message of this enduring love came through Jesus Christ."

I find it quite comforting that in Matthew 16:18 Jesus said to Peter, "You are the Rock on which my church will be built." Then five verses later Jesus said to Peter, "Get out of my sight, Satan!" Later, of course, Peter lied and said he did not know Jesus (Matthew 26:72). Yet Peter was indeed the Rock on which the Christian church was built. God never gave up on Peter even though Peter at times gave up on God and allowed Satan to rule his heart, and, out of fear, denied knowing Jesus. That's comforting to me because I at times have failures similar to that. So part of my faith is that God won't give up on me either.

Even in Paul's time, as can be seen in reading his various letters, there was debate about whether salvation was a result of good works or faith, and that debate continues today. Of course, quotes from the Bible support both views. But it seems to me that Jesus most often portrayed the Father as a loving, merciful father. Jesus most clearly states His view when point blank asked, "What can we do to accomplish the works of God?" Jesus said, "This is the work of God: have faith in the One whom he sent" (John 6:28–29). To me, that verse means believing in the message of Jesus that God loves us and will forgive us when we mess up.

Hmm ...

—How do you see faith and good works in your life?

—What rules are the most important ones? Or do you have to obey them all?

—If we sin after we become Christians, can we still be saved?

—Have you ever given up on God? How did that feel?

*chapter five*

# Confessing Our Sins

A few years ago, I went with some other social workers from my agency to the state institution for people with intellectual disabilities, to visit some of the residents living there who were originally from the county in which we worked. Four residents were going to be discharged from the institution to a supervised apartment program in our county. We needed to take them into a nearby town for medical testing that the institution could not do. We picked up the four residents and went to the nearby town to the medical specialist's office.

As I was driving on the way back, just before getting on the interstate, I turned onto a frontage road instead of the on ramp that led to the interstate. I soon realized my mistake and slammed on the brakes, shouting, "Oh no!" One of the residents said, "What's happened? What's wrong?"

I realized I was upsetting the residents; so, I quickly calmed down and quietly said, "Oh, nothing, we just made a wrong turn, that's all. It's no big deal." The resident responded with,

"Whaddaya mean, *we* made a wrong turn!? I thought *you* was drivin'!"

The moral of the story is that even people with intellectual disabilities can be smart alecks.

Okay, that's not *really* the moral of the story, but it's one of them. The real moral of the story is that we should accept responsibility for our actions. Okay, okay, *I* should accept responsibility for *my* actions. Maybe you already do.

Some of you reading this are probably not old enough to remember *The Flip Wilson Show*, but he had a comedy sketch on the show nearly every week that featured a character that was famous for screeching in a high-pitched voice, "The devil made me do it!" every time he got caught doing something he was not supposed to do. It got to be a popular phrase among my age group if we had to confess a wrong. We'd say, "The devil made me do it." If we got caught in a lie, "The devil made me do it." If we got mad and broke something, "The devil made me do it."

That tendency to blame it on the devil goes way back. It goes all the way back to Adam and Eve. When God discovered that Adam and Eve had eaten of the forbidden fruit and confronted them, Adam blamed his wife, which is what most husbands do. And Eve, instead of saying, "I wanted to be God," said, "the devil made me do it," or words to that effect. (See Genesis 3:1–13.)

For some reason, it's really hard to say, "I messed up." The thing is, you might as well say it, because God knows it. You cannot lie to God; you cannot even just hide the truth from God. You might just as well 'fess up to the mess up. And if God knows the truth, what's the harm in telling a person such as your spouse or friend? What can they do to you that's worse than what God can do to you? But sometimes it seems easier to fess up to God than to a person. Of course it could be that God is more understanding and more able than human beings to forgive.

In the book *Blue Like Jazz*, the author tells the story of building a "confession booth" with his small group of Christians during one of those wild campus festivals at his college. Except when people came to the booth to see what was going on, perhaps considering making a confession, they were surprised. Instead of expecting visitors to step in and confess their sins, the Christians running the booth confessed *their* sins. They confessed that, as followers of Jesus, they had not been very loving but had been judgmental and hateful and apologized for that. They apologized to those who came to their booth for neglecting the poor and lonely and for not helping the sick. That night resulted in that small group of Christians turning into large groups of people that worked on programs for the homeless and having four different Bible study groups of people who were not yet Christians but wanted to learn more about what the Bible had to say.

People are impressed when somebody has the courage to say, "I messed up," rather than, "The devil made me do it."

Hmm …

—It is said that "confession is good for the soul." Have you ever confessed something and felt better for it?

—Have you ever confessed something and had a bad experience as a result?

—Do you think it's possible that some things might be "good for the soul" but not for the body? (Here's an example: One time as a teenager I had to confess that I got a speeding ticket while driving my parents' car. I had to confess because I didn't have the money to pay for the ticket. I was grounded for a month.)

# chapter six

# Love Songs

As I am writing this right now, it is February, and you know what that means: Valentine's Day! I mean there are hearts and Cupids and boxes of chocolates everywhere you look. Love is in the air, and I am in a romantic mood. And my mind was meandering not too long ago about what it would be like if we loved God in a more "romantic" way.

Think of some of the words in the great love songs. "The very thought of you makes my heart sing/Like an April rain in the early spring." Or, "Gayer than laughter are you/Sweeter than music are you/Angel and lover are you/Heaven and earth are you to me." And, "There was love all around/But I never heard it singing/No I never heard it at all/Till there was you." And of course, in honor of the season, how could we forget: "My funny Valentine/Sweet comic Valentine/You make me smile with my heart." Wow! Romantic love is such a powerful emotion.

I can remember some of my first experiences at being in love. I know, it's hard to believe I can remember that far back, but I can.

I would get home from school, usually just in time for dinner because I'd be in some sports practice until late, then I would hurry and eat, and I couldn't wait to go call my girlfriend on the phone. My mom once said, "I don't know how you can be with that girl all day and come home and still have anything left to talk about." Of course, as soon as she said that, I had to go tell my girlfriend about it. I felt like I needed to talk over *every* thing with her.

So I was thinking that if we fell in love, as in romantically, with God, we would think thoughts about God such as, "The very thought of you makes my heart sing," and "You make me smile with my heart." And there would be this sense that you could hardly stand to be separated from God your Lover, and you would want to talk to God about *every* thing.

Somebody once asked Jesus what was the greatest of all the commandments. Jesus said it was this one: "You shall love the Lord, your God, with all your heart, with all your soul, and with all your mind" (Matthew 22:37). That's loving in every way possible, including romantically.

So then I began wondering just how a person can fall in love with God. We don't, after all, just decide to fall in love with a person and then do it. How do you make yourself fall in love? Do you fall in love with somebody because you like the way he or she looks? That's going to make it hard to fall in love with God, because I'm not even sure what God looks like. We can be attracted to people at first because of their looks, but usually falling in love comes after we get to know somebody.

Maybe we have to get to know God in order to fall in love. One of the cool things about being in love is that feeling of *being* loved.

Sometimes I look in the mirror when I get up in the morning and look at the flab and moles and warts and wonder how my wife could possibly love me. But if falling in love were only for the movie star perfect specimens, there wouldn't be much lovin' going on. It's comforting to know that if somebody really loves you, they love you warts and all.

And, of course, the Master at loving us warts and all is God. I think the more we get to know God, the more we experience that feeling of being loved warts and all, it becomes almost impossible *not* to fall in love with God.

Hmm …

—What's your favorite love song? Can you imagine singing that to God?

—Have you ever been loved just for who you are? How did that feel?

—Do you think God loves you just the way you are, or do you need to change something?

—If you must get to know somebody to love them, how do you get to know God?

—What do you love most about God?

# *chapter seven*

## Squirrels and Nuts

I was going for a walk in the park the other day when I saw two squirrels chasing each other around a tree trunk. They stopped when they noticed me and started chattering. My mind started meandering, and I imagined that they were having a conversation about me that went something like this:

Squirrel 1: It's one of those WOHL things.

Squirrel 2: What's a WOHL?

1: Walks on hind legs.

2: Oh. Right. What do you suppose it's doing?

1: Who knows? Those creatures are so sad. They apparently can't really go anywhere except on that hard path where nothing grows. I've never seen one in a tree. Well, I once saw one of the little ones try to go up a tree, but it fell down before it got very far.

2: Yeah. They are sad. I wouldn't want to be them. I've seen them get eaten by a WORT several times.

1: What's a WORT?

2: Walks on round things. (For human readers, that would be an automobile, into which people enter after the doors are opened.) It's like the WOHLs don't even care about getting eaten. They just stand there until the WORT opens its mouth and sucks them in. I don't understand it. You gotta wonder why God even made WOHLS. Okay. I gotta go. I told the mate that I would get five more nuts before dark. See you.

And then they took off. Busy, busy. Squirrels obviously have a limited understanding of humans.

I suppose because it says in Genesis 1:26 that humans were to have "dominion" over the animals, we think that animals are inferior beings. On the other hand, we were given dominion over animals before we messed up and got kicked out of the Garden of Eden. So I don't know. If I were going to create the perfect being, I might add some things to the human being, like eyes in the back of our heads. I sometimes think it would be cool to be able to run up and down a tree like a squirrel. And I think it would be great to be able to fly like an eagle or swim like a dolphin.

It might even be neat to be a cat. Somebody once said that they thought cats were aliens from outer space that invaded earth long ago and made servants out of the human race. I mean, have you ever known a cat that had to work for a living? Okay, okay, I guess farm cats have to earn their keep by catching mice; but that's a pretty low percentage. Most cats just lie around all day, and we feel blessed if they allow us to give them a massage.

Then there are dogs. Remember: *dog* is just *God* spelled backward. Talk about a creature that is capable of unconditional love. It might be a good thing that God is more like a dog than a human being. I mean, we can yell at God if things don't go right, we can ignore Him as we go about our business, and we can be mean to each other, and, still, He loves us.

Yes, I think there's a lot we could learn from watching animals.

However, I've seen dogs get out of control at times. Our neighbor was outside one day with his husky in the front yard, and a person was walking a little pug on the sidewalk across the street. Suddenly the husky jumped up, took off across the street, and attacked the pug, grabbing it by the neck and shaking it like a rag doll. Fortunately, the pug did not die, but it was seriously injured, and the neighbor had to pay a couple thousand dollars for the pug's vet bill. It was a real puzzle as to why the husky, who had always been a friendly and loving dog, was out of control.

Have you ever watched the nature shows on TV where you see lions attacking a herd of antelope? I cringe when I see that one of the antelope is old or injured and can't keep up with the herd. That's the one the lions always go for. I can't even watch that stuff.

The interesting thing is that when we see this type of thing happen, most of us don't see the animals as evil. We often say, "Well, that's the way nature is." The predators have to have something to eat. And it's not as if they don't fight their own species either. The males are often shown to be fighting each other over the females. If humans hunt and kill animals for food, we don't say that it's evil, but if we kill just for fun, out of anger, or a general disregard for life; we say it's evil. Humans have developed rules governing the killing of other humans; and there are times when it is considered evil to kill other humans. I guess maybe humans are supposed to be better than animals, but …

Who told us we were naked?

Hmm …

—Do you think humans are better in God's eyes than animals? If yes, how so? If no, why not?

—Do you think animals have souls and go to Heaven? If so, do they have to be obedient and follow certain standards of behavior?

—How do you interpret the Bible when God says, "Let us make human beings in our likeness, after our image."?

—Can an evil act have a good result? Can a good act end up with evil results? How do we know what is good and what is evil?

# chapter eight

## Growing Old

Those of you who know me might be surprised to learn that I just celebrated my seventieth birthday. I know I don't look a day over forty even though I have white hair, but it's true; I am now seventy years old. I'm in what they call the "autumn of life," meaning, I guess, that my body is starting to chill.

I am now of the age that in a hostage situation, I would be one of the first ones released. It's scary when your body starts to make the same noises as the coffee maker. I'm so old, I can sing along with the elevator music. These days, I am cautioned to slow down by the doctor instead of the highway patrol. But what really bothers me is that now I've been around long enough to know all the answers, but nobody asks me the questions. Plus I feel like my body is really getting out of control. So I decided to join a fitness class for seniors. I bent over, twisted, gyrated, jumped up and down, and perspired for over half an hour. But by the time I got my gym clothes on, the class was over.

Well, okay, if you don't laugh about it, you cry. For some reason this birthday, more than others, has started me thinking about death. I know Christians are supposed to look forward to dying and going to Heaven, but there is still something frightening about it for me. Maybe it's because I enjoy life too much. Maybe if I suffered more, if I were hungry or sick all of the time, or had lost loved ones, for example, maybe I'd be ready to leave.

It's kind of like the little girl who was having a little separation anxiety about going to kindergarten. Her mom said, "You'll like it, honey. You'll have fun all day." The little girl said, "But I already have fun all day at home, Mommy." Maybe I just need to grow up. After all, in Romans 8, it says, "The concern of the flesh is death, but the concern of the spirit is life and peace."

Maybe it's that I just enjoy the things of the flesh too much. I enjoy eating, I enjoy driving an air-conditioned car, I enjoy riding my bicycle, I enjoy banging on the drums, I enjoy hugs and kisses, and so on. I will miss these things that are the "fleshy" part of life, I think. I'm like that little girl: I don't want to die and go to Heaven because I already have fun here. Maybe if I were more spiritually mature, I'd be able to face moving on.

Sometimes getting old is referred to as being "over the hill." One thing I've noticed is that once I got "over the hill" and started down the other side, I picked up speed. Time seems to fly by now. When I was fourteen, I couldn't wait to be sixteen and get my driver's license. It seemed that two years was such a long time. When I was sixteen, I wanted to be eighteen so I could be considered legally an adult. When I was eighteen, I wanted to be twenty-one so I could drink. When I was twenty-one, I wanted to get out of the army and get a job. When I was young, I always wanted time to move along so I could move to the next phase of my life. Going up the hill seemed to take a long time. Nowadays, I just want time to slow down.

It might be that I am not so afraid of dying as I am of getting older. Because I've noticed that there comes a time when things of the flesh are truly *not* enjoyable—when getting out of bed becomes a chore.

My dad died of Alzheimer's disease, and my mom died as a result of two brain surgeries and, at the time of her death, had a third tumor growing in her brain. They both ended their lives in a nursing home. Mom was in pain most of the time, and Dad maybe did not feel pain, but what he did feel and see is anybody's guess. Clearly they were not happy about life toward the end of it. They were ready to move on. I suppose, if we don't die a sudden death due to some accident or disease, we all get to that point. So I'm still at the point where I can laugh at jokes about growing old. Maybe when I get a little older, and life is more suffering than pleasure, I will be ready to go.

There was an article about the great preacher Billy Graham in *Newsweek* magazine not too long ago. He was talking about the trials of old age not long before he died at the age of ninety-nine. He was quoted as saying something that expressed my feelings pretty well. He said, "All my life I've been taught how to die; nobody ever taught me how to grow old."

Hmm …

—Would you rather die and go to Heaven now, or wait awhile?

—What do you think it would take for you to be "ready to go."

—Is it okay to like living and not want to die?

—It you went to a class on how to grow old, what topics would you want covered? Would the focus be on earthly wants or spiritual needs? How are they different?

# chapter nine

## Caterpillars and Butterflies

Bugs give me the willies. Do you know what the willies are? It's when you see something that makes your skin crawl and makes the hair on the back of your neck stand up. I think if we were covered with hair, and if we got the willies, we'd look like a cat that had just been scared, with the hair standing up on our backs. Anyway, bugs give me the willies.

I believe in capital punishment for bugs. If they come into my house, they commit a crime punishable by death. My wife, however, does not believe in capital punishment for bugs. Everybody in our family remembers the story of one Christmas when it was twenty below zero outside, and a ladybug decided it was a lot warmer on my Christmas present than in the window. So she flew down right in front of me and landed on the present. I started to take my napkin and squash it, but my wife screamed, "Wait!" She then carefully cupped the ladybug in her hands and carried it to the front door and opened her hands, gently tossing the ladybug up so the ladybug could fly to freedom.

Since outside it was twenty below zero, the ladybug got about six inches, promptly froze to death, and did a nose-dive onto the front porch. Everybody teases her about the time she killed a ladybug trying to save it from me.

Knowing that I dislike bugs the way I do, you might ask why I would go to a movie called *BUGS!* It's also a mystery to me as to why I did that. I even went to see it at one of those IMAX movie theaters. Those are the theaters with movie screens the size of a football field. So we got to know several bugs up close and personal, and they were huge. They must have had teensy weensy cameras because they were able to shoot these close ups of bugs and make them fill the screen. I almost threw my neck out of joint trying to take in all of Chris Caterpillar from one end of the giant screen to the other.

We were able to watch Chris Caterpillar being born, growing up, and then entering a cocoon and changing into a butterfly. That's when my mind started meandering.

I watched very carefully to see if there was any sign of the caterpillar left as part of the butterfly. There wasn't. The wings were a different color from the caterpillar's body, the legs were totally different, everything was new. Chris Caterpillar became a totally new being. And I thought, "Wow! That's kind of like dying." Chris's wife and kids never saw him again, and I'm sure they missed him. To them he was long gone, and it was a very sad time.

But to Chris, well, it must have been Heaven to him. I mean, as a caterpillar, his whole world was pretty much one tree, and he spent a lifetime plodding around trying to eat all of the hundreds of leaves on that one tree. But now his world was the sky and all

Craig Wood

of the trees in the forest, and he could go anywhere he wanted to go, seemingly by magic.

That started me thinking about how maybe death isn't such a bad thing. We get all upset about people dying and beat our chests and ask how God can allow such a thing. We pray for people to be allowed to live. But maybe when we die, we do something like turn into a butterfly. We really don't know much about what we are like when we go to Heaven. When asked about a woman that had seven different husbands before she died who her husband would be in Heaven, Jesus said there is no marriage in Heaven; we are not like people; we become as angels (Matthew 22:23–30). Unfortunately, He did not say exactly what angels are like. Maybe there just aren't the words.

I have come to the conclusion that angels are about as different from human beings as butterflies are from caterpillars. So that must be a *good* thing, don't you think?

Hmm …

—What do you think it means that "there is no marriage in Heaven; we become as angels."?

—When you envision angels, what comes to mind? What is their purpose? What do they do? What kind of social life do they have?

—What about that woman who had seven husbands die before she did? If she loved all seven of them, what happens in Heaven?

# chapter ten

# The Easter Bunny Vs. Santa

The thing I like about the Easter Bunny is that he doesn't make a list and check it twice, trying to find out who's naughty or nice. Everybody gets an egg or two. But we have to search for the hidden eggs, and some are hard to find. Yet a lot of the eggs are in plain sight, and even the little kids find some, so nobody is left out. Here's what I liked about the Easter Bunny: I didn't have to worry about being naughty. I didn't have to spend the night before Easter worrying about whether I had been good enough. I just always knew the Easter Bunny was going leave something.

Santa is a little scary to me, making that list and checking it twice. I'm nice—oh, maybe 99 percent of the time—but, still, I could probably get caught if the list is checked closely. I usually start trying to be on my best "nice" behavior around October or November, thinking Santa might forget about the stuff I did in August and September. Does anybody know exactly when Santa starts making that list? I'd like to know that. It would help me plan my schedule.

Craig Wood

Of course, the truth is that we shouldn't be nice just to get presents. We should be nice all year round just because, well, it's nice to be nice.

As I was thinking about this, my mind started meandering about the concept of grace, which is sort of the idea that God doesn't make a list and check it twice to see if we have been naughty or nice. God loves us in a way that we can't even fathom because we are his children, not just because we are nice. A lot of us have been taught that we have to behave a certain way in order to receive God's grace. But I think that the Bible seems to teach that God's grace, that love of God that is our salvation, is a gift. It's not something we earned, like a paycheck.

God is like the prodigal son's father. The prodigal son was *really* naughty, and Santa would have had him on the naughty list. But this son eventually came to his senses, and he trusted that his father would treat him at least as well as he treated his hired hands. He headed home with his tail tucked between his legs ready to apologize for all the naughty things he had done and ask for a place in the hired hands shack. But the father was not interested in the list of naughty things; he only knew that his son who was lost was now home. And he threw a party and treated the son like a king (Luke 15:11–32).

Now the brother who was nice all this time and stayed home was a little taken aback and jealous of the attention his brother was getting. It kind of sounded like he was being nice just to get "presents." He was unable to express the grace toward his brother that their father did. Because he had no joy in the return of his younger brother and had only jealousy that there was a party for the brother, he revealed that he was, in fact, just as lost as the younger brother, only in a different way. If we think we deserve our salvation and look down on those who have yet to hear the good news, we are still as lost as that elder brother. The good news is that the Father seeks the elder son as well and urges him to join the party.

The good news Jesus tells us about is that God is really more like the Easter Bunny, bringing us eggs without checking on the naughty and nice. The egg is a symbol of new life, or of life's potential, waiting to be born. Jesus comes offering us this new life—a chance to be reborn. He comes to help us come to our senses, as did the prodigal son, and help us to know that our Father in Heaven loves us not because we behave a certain way but because we are His children.

So I really like Easter because I feel important and happy and saved, not because of anything I did, but because I am loved.

And besides all that, I *really* like chocolate.

Hmm ...

—Are you more like the prodigal son or the good son? What makes you think that?

—If you are a parent, do you love your children because of the way that they behave or despite their misbehavior? How do you communicate that message to them?

*chapter eleven*

---

# The New Tower of Babel

---

I was looking at the full moon the other night, and it seemed close enough to touch. My mind started meandering, and I thought, "How many guys can say they have been there and stepped on the surface of that thing?" I looked it up. Just twelve men have walked on the surface of the moon. Six of them drove the lunar rover. It seems like a miracle that we could do that. And we did it around fifty years ago with almost primitive computer equipment. When we really put our minds to it, we humans can accomplish about anything we want to.

In fact, God said that same thing, sort of. There is a story in Genesis about the "Tower of Babel," in which the people of Earth, who the story says at that time all spoke the same language, were making great technological progress. They had learned how to make bricks and harden them so that they could construct great tall buildings. They decided to build a great city with a tower that would reach to the sky. Perhaps they thought they would be able to reach God, since they believed that God lived above the clouds. God saw what was happening and said, "If now, while they are one people, all speaking the same language, and they have started to do this, nothing will later stop them from doing whatever they presume to do. Let us then go down and there confuse their language, so that one will not understand what another says" (Genesis 9:1–11).

Thus began our communication problems. When I remembered this story, my mind naturally started meandering. I was thinking that a lot of our problems with other countries in the world occur because we really can't communicate very well. Then I thought, "Even when we all speak English, we don't communicate very well, as in Republicans and Democrats." Then I thought, "Men and women don't even communicate all that well," and it's because men are from Mars and women are from Venus, or so I've been told.

For example, my wife sometimes says, "Are you going to wear that shirt to work today?" Since I have it on, and I'm ready to head out the door, it seems to me the answer is obvious. What she really means is, "That shirt does not go with your pants, and you need to change." And then there's "Did you leave that light on in the basement for a reason?" Translation: "Get down to the basement and turn the light off." Of course, she, on the other hand, has trouble understanding me when she asks, "How much time is left in the game?" and I say, "fifty-three seconds," which means it will be about half an hour before the game is over if you include the commercials, time-outs, and instant replay reviews.

There is also the age gap. We were visiting at my daughter's house the other day, and my two-year-old granddaughter was sitting in her high chair and said to me, "Canoe yet key bob pup?" Not having a clue as to what was just said to me, I looked at her mother for the translation. It was, "Can you let Caleb up?" Caleb is the cat, and the door to the basement was closed, so the cat was meowing wanting up from the basement. I was the closest to the door. It was good that I had a translator, or I would not have known what I was supposed to do, or even that a request was being made.

When the internet came into being, I thought, "Great, this is it. The common translator. People will be able to communicate. We can become one human race, stop wars, and have peace." But no. For some reason, world peace did not happen, even with the invention of the internet. I now believe we live in a time of the new Tower of Babel. There almost seems to be more dissension than ever. It's kind of like the marriage counselor who told the couple being counseled that they needed to communicate more. When they came in for the next appointment, the counselor asked if they had communicated. The wife said, "Yes. He said he was tired of my nagging, and I told him to straighten up and fly right." Communication might not always be the problem.

But the good news is that even though it was apparently God who gave us a variety of languages, He also gave us a solution to the problem: love. Without God's spirit of love and kindness, we do not cooperate, and we often can't communicate, even if we do speak the same language. Paul put it this way: "If I speak in human and angelic tongues, but do not have love, I am a resounding gong or clashing cymbal" (1 Corinthians 13:1). Thus, we can't accomplish the things we need to just by being able to speak the same language. But because of love, my wife and I have been married for fifty years despite that she is from Venus, and I am from Mars. Trust me, I believe in miracles because it's a miracle that she has put up with me that long.

Somehow, I think we would communicate better if we all "loved our neighbor as ourselves," which Jesus said in Matthew 22:39 was one of the two greatest commandments. If we could be a little more meek, a little more full of grace, and a little more Christlike, who knows what miracles God could accomplish through us?

Hmm ...

—What do you think is the point of the story of the Tower of Babel?

—Now that differing languages is not an obstacle, what keeps humans from acting as one?

—How can we overcome cultural or ethnic differences to improve communication?

—Does "social media" contribute to or detract from better relationships?

—What is meant in the directive to love our neighbors as ourselves?

## chapter twelve

# Power of Prayer

Descriptions of prayer are abundant throughout Christian history. "True prayer," wrote Saint Augustine, "is nothing but love." Prayer should arise from the heart. "Prayer," said Saint John Vianney, "is the inner bath of love into which the soul plunges itself." "Everyone of us needs half an hour of prayer each day," remarked Saint Francis de Sales, "except when we are busy—then we need an hour." Definitions of prayer are important but insufficient. There is a huge difference between knowing about prayer and praying. On this issue, the Rule of Saint Benedict is clear, "If a person wants to pray, let them go and pray."

I was in a hurry the other day. I needed to be someplace in about fifteen minutes, and I couldn't find my keys. We're down to one set of keys, so my wife could not help me. I was running upstairs, downstairs, looking through all my coat pockets, and looking in the dirty clothes hamper in case I had left them in my pants. I mean I was desperate.

So what do you think? Should I be praying for God to help me find my keys? Is that something God really worries about? I know my wife was praying I'd find them. Either that or she was praying I wouldn't destroy the house looking for them. She was praying for something; I couldn't tell exactly what.

I also wonder about praying for victory in a ball game. I figure there are probably Christians on both teams praying for victory; so what's God supposed to do? Is it something on the order of "May the best pray-er win"? Or whoever sinned the least wins? You'd think Christian colleges would never lose a game. Well, unless they played another Christian college. How does God decide? Or maybe He just lets them have at it, and the best athletes win.

Anyway, back to losing my keys, I was thinking maybe I should pray, "Give me this day my daily bread, and while You're at it, help me find my keys … please. In fact, Father, skip the bread part, because I don't have time to eat."

The more I thought about it, though, I began to think that really prayer is not a magic trick. It's not like in the old TV show *Bewitched*, where I could wiggle my nose and make the car start or wiggle my nose and cause a fumble by the opposing team. Have you ever locked your keys in your car? Wouldn't you love to be able to just close your eyes and pray, and then the locks magically click, and the doors open?

One time Jesus went out to the desert and camped out for forty days and nights, except that on this campout, He did not eat. He fasted. So he was pretty hungry. He was so hungry that the stones were starting to look like dinner rolls. We're talking about a guy who could multiply a handful of fish and a few loaves of bread into enough food to feed five thousand people. So he was tempted to pray those stones into bread. In fact, Matthew 4:3 says the devil tempted Jesus and said, "If you're the Son of God, command that these stones become loaves of bread." That was when Jesus said, "It is written, 'One does not live by bread alone, but by every word that comes forth from the mouth of God'" (Matthew 4:4).

On the other hand, in Luke 11:9 it is also written, "Ask, and you will receive; seek and you will find." So I don't necessarily think it's wrong to pray for help in finding keys. I'm just not sure about it. One of the messages in the *Lord of the Rings* movie was that the power of the rings could be both your salvation and your undoing.

The power of prayer might be something like that. It might be all about where your heart is.

Anyway, when I prayed for God to help me find my keys, I thought I heard Him say something like my Mom used to say: "If you had put them where they belong, you'd know where they are."

Hmm ...

—Do you think I should have been praying for God to help me find my keys?

—Does God look for lost items, help you find a perfect mate, win ball games, cure diseases?

—Why aren't all prayers answered?

—How does the Lord's prayer help us?

*chapter thirteen*

# No Control at the Airport

Recently, my wife and I took our first ever spring break vacation in which we went south to warmer weather. It reminded me of a movie I saw many years ago when I was a teenager about teenagers leaving a snowstorm in Chicago to take spring break in Florida. Actually, instead of going to Florida, we went to visit my wife's sister in a retirement village in Yuma, Arizona. And instead of dancing to rock 'n' roll on the beach, we played dominoes in a mobile home with a bunch of gray hairs like me. But it was fun—until it was time to come back to Iowa, that is.

We were sitting in the airport in Phoenix expecting to be home with an hour to spare before bedtime, when we heard those dreaded words: "Ladies and gentleman, we have just been informed that Flight 7864 from Phoenix to Denver (that would be *our* flight) has been delayed for three hours due to mechanical difficulties. If your connection in Denver will be leaving before your scheduled arrival, you will need to rebook that flight. Oh. And we would like to thank you for flying the friendly skies."

When my wife returned from the ladies room about ten minutes later, she said to clueless me, "Honey, I think you need to be standing in that line over there to see about getting another flight out of Denver." I was determined to be a model of calm, just hoping somebody would ask me how I could be so calm so I could then say, "I am a child of God; I don't sweat the small stuff, and everything is small stuff. God will provide." (Don't worry; I wouldn't really say that.)

I did relatively well in this line. It was interesting watching the reactions of others, though. Some people were really upset with the airline.

"They should just get another plane."

"They need more help at the counter."

"Why can't they just hold up the flight in Denver. There are, like, ten of us here that are going to get on that plane."

"No wonder this outfit's bankrupt."

Some people were really upset with other people. "If that guy doesn't hurry up, I'm going to personally give him a one-way ticket out of here."(The person in question had been at the counter for an hour arguing with an agent about what alternate flights to take.) Some poor woman who just seemed to wander in with a general question not even related to the delay got screamed at by a half dozen people: "Hey! The line forms at the rear, lady!"

Some people seemed to delight in having inside knowledge. A man snapped his cellphone shut and whispered to his wife,

"Okay, I just got off the phone with my travel agent, and she says because of spring break there are no flights out of Denver for two days, but she's going to try to reroute us through Kansas City."

But I stayed calm, smiling at people and being pleasant. Nobody asked me how I could do it, though; so I never had a chance to witness. They probably thought there was something wrong with me, standing there for over two hours, smiling in the midst of this crisis. Yes, I did good in that line.

It was the *next* night in Chicago. I mean, we were supposed to be home at ten o'clock on Saturday night, and by midnight on *Sunday* night, we had only gotten as far as Chicago. Then we heard, "Ladies and gentlemen, Flight 1735 to Cedar Rapids has been canceled due to thunderstorms both here and in Cedar Rapids. You may rebook at the convenient customer service centers located near Gate 12 or Gate 3." I was all done smiling. I was too tired to smile. Maybe it's all small stuff, but it was wearing me out. Now I was getting angry.

Fortunately, while we were standing in line at one of the "convenient customer service centers," we started talking to another couple headed for Cedar Rapids. One of them worked for a business with a contract with a car rental place, and, after a few phone calls, he was able to find a rental car and invited us to ride home with them. We headed for Cedar Rapids and got home at six o'clock Monday morning. God provided us those two people at least, or, for all I know, we'd *still* be in Chicago.

The thing I took away from all this was how it feels to be in a situation over which you have absolutely no control. We were at the mercy of forces beyond our control: the airlines, the weather, other people. It was not a good feeling, but the reality is that there is much in life over which we have no control. One of the things we need to learn how to do in life is learn how to deal with that "not in control" feeling.

God keeps trying to tell us we are not in control. Yet we, or at least I, keep thinking we are.

Hmm ...

—How do you feel when you discover that you can't control a situation? Surprised? Worried? Angry?

—Is God in control of all situations? What is your role?

—What helps when you are in a chaotic situation? What might make it more difficult?

*chapter fourteen*

# God Is in Control

One time we were on our way to church, which involves driving a few miles on a highway, when our paths crossed with a young buck deer. It was broad daylight, and that buck should have been taking a nap. But he was either after a mate or running from a hunter because he did not look both ways before crossing the road. The collision cost him his life, and it cost me (well, it cost the insurance company) $7,500 in damages to my minivan.

We are grateful that we suffered no injuries. We know a person who lost an eye in just such a collision when the shattered windshield flew into her face. Our windshield shattered but did not fly into our faces. So the worst was that the van suffered body damage, which can be repaired.

But my mind started meandering as we sat there waiting for the tow truck. I wondered why God didn't want us to go to church that day. Maybe the sermon was going to be bad, and God figured I didn't need to hear it. No. That couldn't be. I had better get the video of the sermon and see what I missed. Then I began to think about whether God really does make bad things happen to people. Well, that topic is too big for this chapter. Whole books have been written about that.

Mark Twain once said, "Plan for the future; it's where you're going to spend the rest of your life." That sounds pretty smart, except that Jesus said, "Do not worry about tomorrow; tomorrow will take care of itself. Sufficient for a day is its own evil"(Matthew 6:34). And James, who seems to be a pretty angry fellow most of the time in his writing, takes it even further and says that if you say, "Today or tomorrow we shall go into such and such a town, spend a year there doing business, and make a profit," you are being arrogant and boastful and even evil. He says we should say instead, "If the Lord wills it, we shall live to do this or that" (James 4:13–17). Or I suppose you could say what my Grandpa used to say: "If the Lord's willin', and the creek don't rise."

During the coronavirus pandemic, Robert Samuelson wrote in the *Washington Post* that we tend to think that with all our technology and scientific progress, we are in control. He pointed out that we did not anticipate jetliners being hijacked and crashed into skyscrapers; we did not anticipate the financial meltdown of 2008, and many still do not think climate change is a problem. He said that despite our technological progress, "The reality is that our control over the future is modest at best, nonexistent at worst. We react more to events than lead them. We worship at the altar of progress without adequately acknowledging its limits."

Maybe we need to have the George Burns attitude. When George Burns was traveling around at age ninety-nine (almost one hundred!) doing his comedy routine, he would open his act by saying, "Good evening, ladies and gentlemen. It's good to be here. At my age it's good to be anywhere."

Okay, I'm guilty. I'm guilty because I had told my daughter we would be at church for the late service and then go out to lunch, assuming that I had complete control over my life. Hah!

I think most of us like to think we're in control of our lives. We like to think that if we are well off, it is because of wise decisions that we made and good planning that we did. The fact is, if we are well off, we need to realize we are just truly fortunate.

Jesus said that God "makes his sun rise on the bad and the good, and causes rain to fall on the just and the unjust" (Matthew 5:45).

We might have worked hard to get where we are, but we could have worked just as hard, been hit by a truck, and become disabled. Or we could have been born in Syria instead of the United States and become one of the million plus in terrible refugee camps. Many things impact our lives that are completely out of our control. As most farmers know, we definitely do not control the sun and the rain.

When I can get hold of the TV remote control before my wife, I feel very powerful. Though we might think we have the power in this world and control over our lives, we need to remember that God's got the remote.

Hmm ...

—What do you think Jesus was saying when He said God "causes rain to fall on the just and the unjust."?

—Since God is in control, does that mean a person ought to stop trying, or stop working for a better future?

—Is it possible to be partners with God on your life's path?

—Do you "worship at the altar of progress?"

## chapter fifteen

# Acts of God

Not many people know this, but the Sony Corporation believes in God. I figured this out the other day when I was reading the warranty card that came with my new DVD player. I recently had to use the warranty on an item to have it repaired, so when I opened this new box, I thought I'd read the warranty just in case. So, I got out my magnifying glass and put it up against the small print.

The warranty says, "This warranty does not cover cosmetic damage or damage due to acts of God, accident, misuse, abuse, negligence, commercial use, or modification to any part of the product." I figured if they believed their product could be damaged by an "act of God," they must believe in God. Naturally, my mind meandered over to this: "What do they mean by acts of God?" Is that like bursting into flames for no reason, as in the burning bush? I also wondered if Sony would cover acts of the devil, since there was no disclaimer on that. I would like to discuss that with them.

I might tell them that God doesn't make bad things happen, so if the machine breaks, it must be the act of the devil, not God. Therefore, they need to pay me back my money.

Also, United Airlines believes in God. When we were stranded in the Chicago airport last spring due to a thunderstorm, I asked the lady behind the desk if they were going to put us up in a hotel since there were no more flights that night. She said that they did not do that if the flight was canceled due to an act of God. I told her God didn't make it storm; Mother Nature did, so how about the hotel? I then smiled in a hurry because she looked like she might be ready to call security.

I think it's interesting that some companies talk about acts of God as if they really know what an act of God is. I wonder if atheists could get their money back for those things since they don't believe in God, which logically means that they don't believe there is any such thing as an act of God.

And the truth of the matter is that God does make bad things happen. Or at least God makes things happen that we think are bad. It seems to have been God's intention that Jesus hang on the cross for us to be saved. I'm sure if we had been there during the crucifixion, we would have been convinced that Jesus hanging on the cross was a bad thing. In fact, we might have thought that things could get no worse. Our leader was being taken from us—the one we believed would conquer our enemies. We could not have known then that Jesus would conquer our enemies in ways we could not imagine.

In fact, when Jesus was telling the disciples that He was going into Jerusalem and would be killed, Peter said, "No way!" (Or words to that effect. See Matthew 16:22.) Peter thought Jesus getting killed would be a bad thing. I mean, you can't really fault the guy for that. But what happened was that Jesus called Peter Satan for even having such thoughts. He said to Peter, "You are not thinking as God does, but as humans do" (Matthew 16:23). Poor Peter! I'm sure he said what he did out of love and concern for Jesus. Yet Jesus became angry. So, I don't know. Trying to figure out what are acts of God might be dangerous.

Concerning warranties and guarantees, in my opinion the best guarantee ever known *is* an act of God: the act of grace and truth that came through Jesus Christ.

Hmm ...

—Can you name some acts of God? Do they share commonalities? Do they affect a few people or a lot of people?

—Do you think storms or other natural catastrophes such as pandemics are acts of God?

—Do you think accidents (such as the kind that might cause damage to a DVD player) are acts of God?

—Do you know how other cultures define acts of God?

*chapter sixteen*

# Mothers

April showers lead to May flowers, Cinco de Maya, baseball, hot dogs, apple pie, and Mother's Day. I was thinking about Mother's Day recently and about how the Bible is pretty much a male-dominated society, though there obviously are some significant women mentioned that help bring us the Word of God. But in terms of fathers and mothers, 1,023 verses in the Bible contain the word *father*, and only 291 verses contain the word *mother*. Would you believe I went through the Bible and counted those verses? If you would, would you also be interested in looking at a deed I have for some land on an island in the Pacific? Actually, these days they have computer programs that will count those things up for you. Anyway, the point is that mothers do not get equal press in the Bible.

Nevertheless, mothers are important. Honoring your mother is one of the Ten Commandments; so they must be important. And, as Paul says later on, honoring your mother (and father) is the first commandment with a promise. Honoring your mother will bring you a long life (Ephesians 6:2–3). But if you curse your mother, you must be put to death. It says that right in Exodus 21:17. Wow! That's harsh.

In fact, Deuteronomy 21 says that if a man has a stubborn and rebellious son who does not obey his father and mother and will not listen to them when they discipline him, his father and mother shall take hold of him and bring him to the elders at the gate of his town. "Then all his fellow citizens shall stone him to death" (Deuteronomy 21:21). So even just being disobedient could get you stoned to death. It's a wonder that teenagers survived at all in those days. It's a good thing Jesus came and said that if you are without sin you can cast the first stone. That sort of limits the number of people who could cast a stone. Not that I cursed my mother, but I might have when I was a rebellious teenager. I know I was disobedient on occasion. I'm sure there are times over the years when I did not honor her sufficiently. And the main point is that the Bible says we should honor our mothers.

One of my favorite parables is the story of the prodigal son. That's the one where one of two sons talks his father into selling half his land and giving the money to the son for an early inheritance. The son immediately takes off for the big city to spend his inheritance. So, my meandering mind wonders what the mother said. It probably went something like: "You sold half the land and did *what* with the money?"

Then the kid, after blowing all the money and nearly starving to death, decides he would be better off at home. In my meandering mind, I can see it all now. Mom is peeling potatoes; Dad is washing up, and one of the servants comes and says, "Your son is coming over the hill." Then Dad, trying to impress his wife and not wanting to appear weak, says, "That kid is going to get a whippin'!" But Mother says, "No, honey, we must rejoice. For we have been grieving the loss of our son, and now he has come back to us." And Dad says, "Yup, that's just what I was thinking." The rest is history. (For the *real* version of this story, see Luke 15:11–32.)

The love of mothers for their children is very special. And mothers will forgive a multitude of sins. When Paul wanted to illustrate how he loved the Thessalonians, he said, "We were gentle among you, as a nursing mother cares for her children." A four-year-old once defined love like this: "Love is when you come home, and your puppy licks your face all over even after you left him alone all day."

A mother's love is kind of like that. Even if you borrow money from her and don't pay her back, even if you borrow her car and leave her with an empty gas tank, even if you tell her you'll call and don't, even if you forget her on her birthday or even if you forget her on Mother's Day, when you go home, you get kisses. And the cool thing is that God's love for us is like that too.

Hmm …

—Is it possible to honor mothers who are not perfect? How can we do that?

—Think about a time when you didn't honor your mother. How do you feel about your actions now?

—Think about a time when you didn't honor God. How do you feel about your actions now?

# chapter seventeen

# Some Assembly Required

I like to buy stuff that's already put together. I mean if I see something that is the size of a bicycle on display, then the guy goes and gets me one, and the box is the size of a suitcase, I know I've got a problem. I hate it when the box says, "Some assembly required." Then they usually add the insult on the box, saying, "Can be assembled easily in minutes!" Yeah, right. All you need is a garage full of power tools and a few friends with engineering degrees.

When I put things together at home, it's sort of like an Armageddon: there is much wailing and gnashing of teeth. If I bought a horse that needed to be assembled at home, it would turn out looking like a giraffe.

Back when my kids were little, I especially dreaded buying Christmas gifts that required assembly. That's when the pressure is really on. You can't really put the thing together until Christmas Eve because it might be discovered. So then you can't even start until late that night after the kids have gone to bed, and you know you have to get up early. Pressure. Usually, I was perspiring heavily before I even started.

Typically, I would open the package and read the instructions. (Okay, that was after about five years of trying it without reading the instructions.) The instructions tell me I need a tool that is out in my garage, which at my house means I have to bundle up, put my boots on, and wade through the snow with my flashlight to go to the garage. After looking for half an hour and freezing, I find the tool and go back to the house. Then I can't get the package of screws open and pull and pull until it snaps open, and the screws go flying all over the place, including one going down the heat register. Seriously. This seems to happen every year.

Nope. Putting stuff together is not my favorite thing to do.

That makes it a challenge to become what God wants me to be because I didn't come all put together either. I think we're all that way. When we're born, we all should have little "some assembly required" signs on us.

We come with God-given talents, parts in a box that we have to figure out how to use in order to grow in God's service. God does not want us to sit on our assets, as did the man who buried his one talent. God wants us to step out on the sea and go for it.

Of course, there are instructions. Reading the Bible will provide some direction on how to put ourselves together. There's also the 1-800 tech support line known as prayer that can help. Not that we won't experience some frustration anyway. Because of *our* shortcomings, we tend to start down wrong paths occasionally, we use the wrong tool for the wrong job, the wrong talent for the wrong situation, and we make a mess of ourselves. So, we sometimes must "take a mulligan," as golfers say, and start over.

Once somebody asked me if I had lived in Iowa my entire life. I said, "Not yet." My entire life isn't over yet. I might live in Iowa my entire life, and I might live some of it somewhere else. Working on putting myself together is also not over yet. As Yogi once said, "It ain't over till it's over." We are a work in progress. We're not like a bicycle that is put together, wears out, and is replaced. We're more like a computer that keeps getting upgrades.

So, it's important to keep at it and not give up. As somebody once said, "What you are is God's gift to you; what you become is your gift to God."

Hmm ...

—What kind of "upgrades" have you experienced in your lifetime?

—Can you identify some "instructions" in the Bible that have helped you identify and use your God-given talents?

—Can you think of something you need to work on right now?

chapter eighteen

# Subordinate to Authorities

A country in the Middle East is occupied by the army of the most powerful nation in the world, and the little country's own leaders have little control over their own people. A religious leader begins to emerge, and the existing leadership of the little country seems threatened. The stability of the country, which is shaky to begin with, is said by some to be on the verge of erupting into an outright revolt. This gains the attention of the occupying force. At the urging of the country's own leaders, the occupying army kills the religious leader in hopes of maintaining peace. Little did the Roman soldiers know when they hung Jesus on the cross that His followers would someday rule Rome. Usually things work out the way God intended.

Some people thought Barack Obama was the devil personified, or, if not the devil himself, then at least the devil's tool. Some people thought that George Bush was the devil, or perhaps just controlled by the devil. These are things that we do not discuss during gatherings of my extended family, for fear that a food fight (or worse) might break out.

I was reading through the book of Romans the other day and got into chapter 13, where I was reminded that the Bible says that God placed both Barack Obama and George Bush in their position of ruler. So you can't tell me that God doesn't have a sense of humor. Well, okay, it doesn't mention any names, but it does say, "Let every person be subordinate to the higher authorities, for there is no authority except from God." and "whoever resists authority opposes what God has appointed, and those who oppose it will bring judgment upon themselves" (Romans 13:1–2).

When Saint Paul was writing the book of Romans, the authorities were not Christian. They were not even Jewish. They believed in a bunch of gods but not God. Yet Paul was telling the church in Rome that the Roman authorities were placed there by God. What would we think if the next president was an atheist? Wouldn't Christians have a problem thinking that God thought an atheist ought to be president?

Somebody once said that the reason Satan is so angry all of the time is that whenever he works a particularly clever bit of mischief, God uses it to serve His own righteous purpose. God seems to always be able to outfox the fox even when we think Satan is in control.

My mind started meandering about a recent sermon I heard regarding how our stay here on Earth is so brief relative to our eternity that it is like spending a weekend at a hotel. Mind you, my mind did not meander *during* the sermon, just afterward. If our focus is to be on our eternity, why would we want to get caught up in who is selected to manage the hotel? Oh, I suppose if they ask us to vote on the manager, we could do that. We might approve of the way the current manager is running things, or we might not. But would we want to risk not loving our neighbor who voted for somebody else? Would we want to risk eternity over something that has little bearing on our eternity?

We are fortunate to live in a country where we are free to worship God out in the open, where the debate (among Christians) is not about which God to worship, but how to interpret scripture. But even if we lived in a country where the rulers did not believe in God, we would still be expected to be "subordinate to the authorities." So, if we're not supposed to get angry and yell at each other about politics, how *are* we supposed to focus on our eternity? Well, later on in this same chapter (Romans 13:10) it says, "Love does no evil to the neighbor; hence, love is the fulfillment of the law." It doesn't matter who is managing the hotel. We check in and check out, and while we are here, we love our neighbor. Right?

Hmm ...

—Do you discuss politics at your family gatherings? How does that work?

—Do you think one political party is more Christian than another? What makes you think that?

—Do you think most people at your church are of the same political party?

—Do you feel free to discuss politics at church?

—Why would God put somebody of the "wrong" political party in power?

## chapter nineteen

# Music Is an Offering

Wisdom comes from unexpected places sometimes. The Fifth Army Band in North Chicago performed a lot of "public relations" types of functions to promote a good public image of the army. They did lots of parades in the city of Chicago and suburbs, as well as concerts in the parks and many other special occasions. So, they had a concert choir.

The director of the concert choir was a man who almost always had a cigarette going. When he talked to you, he was constantly in motion, shifting his weight, looking around, or cleaning his glasses. He had a skin condition that made it appear that his face was always peeling from sunburn or something. His vision was poor, so he was always half-squinting. Plus, he would do dumb stuff, like work on his car in subzero weather and freeze the skin on his fingers. In addition to conducting the choir, he was the band's top clarinetist, and it was not good when his fingers couldn't feel the clarinet. You wouldn't think of wisdom coming from this guy, but it did.

I met him shortly after reporting for duty in December 1969. I had completed four years of college, and during the fourth year, I had majored in percussion. In those days you were only allowed four years of college before being required to serve your country. So I auditioned for the Fifth Army Band and was fortunate enough to be selected. Shortly after getting settled in the barracks, I received word that the concert choir director wanted to meet with me. He welcomed me to the concert choir. I told him I was a drummer, not a singer. He told me that if the concert choir were voluntary, he wouldn't have enough singers to do four-part harmony. I said I understood, but I really couldn't sing, and his choir would be better off without me. He said he understood, but he'd look forward to seeing me at the next rehearsal. After I performed with the choir for a couple of months, the director met with me and told me I had the distinction of being the first bandsman to be relieved of concert choir duty. Not only did I sound bad, but I caused other guys to sound bad too.

There was a little church that we attended while stationed in North Chicago. Shortly after we started attending, they lost their choir director. Knowing I was a musician, the pastor asked me if I would be the choir director. I turned the job down, but a little later I said to the army choir director, "You'll never believe this, but our church just asked me to be their choir director," and I laughed thinking it was a good joke.

He asked, "What's so funny about that?" No sense of humor, this guy.

I said, "Well, as you know, I can't sing."

And he said, "But you're probably the most knowledgeable person in the congregation about music, or they wouldn't have asked you. And you don't have to sing; you have to direct."

Being a relatively new Christian and therefore being thoroughly self-righteous and judgmental, I said, "Well, besides, I think it's wrong to be giving performances in church. It ought to be learning about God, and that's it."

He said, "I don't see it that way. My view is that music helps connect people to God. Music touches the spirit in people, even secular music. That's why throngs of people go to concerts, are moved to dancing, and yelling, and oftentimes moved to tears. And worship music does that in a spiritual way to help people to connect to God. The choir is an offering that leads people in that experience."

"An offering?" I asked.

"Yes, it's an offering of the best that the congregation has to offer in the way of music, the first fruits, if you will. Plus, the choir helps the congregation sing better. So, it helps each person in the congregation offer the best that they have to give of their own voices, too."

Great. *Now* he tells me. By the time I decided to take the job, they had given it to somebody else. Another one of those times when God rang my doorbell, and I was taking a nap.

Now fast-forward thirty-five years. These days, a lot of churches don't have choirs; they have "worship teams" with guitars and drums and everything. So, since I play drums, I got on a worship team. The musicians on the worship teams often worry about being too prideful, about showing off, about making it a performance. I often hear them pray, "Help to make this service not about us, Lord, but about You." But God wants us to do our best with the talents he gave us. He doesn't want us to hide our light under a bushel basket. And it's probably okay for us to feel good about conquering a difficult piece of music. I think the old army choir director had a good idea. The organist, the choir, and worship teams are an offering of the best music a church has to offer. They are offering up their talents and in addition helping to connect people to God—helping people to offer up their best.

And there are quite a few biblical references to singing, such as Psalm 33:3. "Sing to him a new song; play skillfully on the strings, with a loud shout." This seems to support the choir director's wisdom that music and singing is an offering. And my view is that whether it is classical or contemporary, organ or guitars and drums, music is an offering that helps us to connect with God.

Hmm ...

—Does music touch you in a special way? What do you think about when that happens?

—What are your views on contemporary Christian music?

—What would church be like without any music?

—Is it okay to applaud the musicians in church?

## chapter twenty

# Let the Light Shine

Jack Lemmon once said, "If you have trouble meeting new people, try picking up somebody else's golf ball out on the golf course." I've tried that, and it is definitely a good conversation starter. Of course, the conversation isn't always friendly, but there is conversation. But maybe that's not the best way to meet new people. Maybe it would be better to just get involved in a discussion group at church. If you are reading this book, you might have already done that.

If not, why not? My mind was meandering about this, and I was wondering why people would choose *not* to get involved in a discussion group. I suppose the most common reason is that you'd have to miss your favorite TV show. Or maybe you are like my son, who thought *nobody* could be as messed up as he was and be able to identify with any of his life experiences.

But he discovered this truth: everybody else seems normal ... until you get to know them better. So here's a comforting thought: there are no "normal" people attending churches. Everybody is just a little bit different. So don't worry about being different. If you're different, you fit right in.

When I was in college learning how to be a social worker, one view of human development that we studied was that we are born as little jewels, and sometimes the experiences of childhood cover that jewel with garbage, either from parents or mean kids or just bad luck. And then, when we become adults, we try to cover that garbage with some kind of paint job to present an image that we think is acceptable to whatever group with which we want to associate. When a person has trouble holding that all together and needs counseling, the first thing that a person does in counseling is start peeling away the phony paint job, and what do they see? The garbage that they had covered with paint. It takes a lot of effort to continue the peeling process, strip away the garbage, and get to the jewel.

There's actually some biblical support for that view. I see it in the Adam and Eve story. Adam and Eve were naked and in perfect harmony with creation; they were jewels, until they ate of the Tree of the Knowledge of Good and Evil. Then they covered their nakedness. God's first question to them after they had eaten the forbidden fruit was, "Who told you that you were naked?" (Genesis 3:11).

It is the Snake that causes us to try and hide ourselves from God and from each other. And sometimes we even try to deceive ourselves. We would rather not wade through all of the garbage to get to the jewel. But it is important for mental and spiritual health to uncover the jewel that is the true self and let it shine.

Jesus began His Sermon on the Mount with, "Blessed are the poor in spirit, for theirs is the Kingdom of Heaven" (Matthew

5:3). So, if you are poor in spirit, there is hope: the kingdom of Heaven is yours. Later on in that sermon, He says, "You are the light of the world. Your light must shine before others" (Matthew 5:14–16). The salvation of the world depends on *you*. *You* are the light of the world. When I read that verse not too long ago, I thought, "God help us if the salvation of the world depends on me." Then the thought came to me, "God does help us."

Discussion groups are not therapy sessions, but they might help you learn how to let your light shine. And a discussion group might also help you to help others to let their light shine. There ought to be enough discussion groups that you can find one that meets when you won't have to miss your favorite TV show. And don't worry, everybody there is just as abnormal as you are.

Hmm ...

—Have you ever worried about being different from everybody else in a group? How did you handle that? How can we understand that everybody is a little different?

—What does it mean to you when Jesus says you are the light of the world?

—What specific thing can you, personally, do to let your light shine?

## chapter twenty=one

# Moses and Flaws

Most people know the name Moses. Even a lot of people who don't go to church know the name Moses and the idea of the Ten Commandments. I think Moses has to be one of the most famous names ever, right up there with Babe Ruth and Jackie Robinson. Okay, I know a lot of young people right now are saying, "Babe Who?" Well, like Yogi Berra always said, "You could look it up." Or, as my grandson says, "Google it."

But if Moses would have had his way about things, nobody would have heard of him. Moses was just a lowly shepherd who worked for his father-in-law. His father-in-law was the one who owned the sheep (Exodus 3:1). When Moses heard God say to him, "I am sending you to Pharaoh to bring my people, the Israelites, out of Egypt," Moses did not say, "Okay, I'm on my way." He said "Who am I to go to Pharaoh and bring the Israelites out of Egypt?" (Exodus 3:10–11). In today's lingo, that would be, "Are you kiddin' me? Am I on the Practical Jokers TV program?" And that wasn't the end of it. Moses argued with God about this at various times during their conversations over the next months, saying things like, "Nobody is going to listen to me" (Exodus 6:12). "I have no credentials" (Exodus 4:1). "I have a speech impediment" (Exodus 4:10). "Send somebody else" (Exodus 4:13).

Moses tried his best to get out of it. But God didn't let him off the hook. So, Moses accomplished the task and became famous.

Many of us feel that we have nothing to offer—no skill, no talent, no ability to be of any use to God. So even if we heard God's voice asking us to do something, we might say:

"You are kidding me, right?"
"There's no way I could teach a Sunday school class."
"There's no way I could help people who are in the hospital."
"There's no way I could speak to an addiction recovery group."
"There's no way I could work in the church kitchen without eating all the food."
"Wash dishes? I don't even do my own dishes!" Etc.

But if you think about it, many of the major characters of the Bible were flawed, yet God used them. God used them actually in two ways. He used them to accomplish what He wanted them to accomplish in real time, and He also used them to teach us about Himself thousands of years later.

I saw this on the internet (KeithFerrin.com) the other day and thought it was worth repeating here: The next time you think you can't be of any use to God, remember:

Abraham was too old,
Isaac was a daydreamer,
Jacob was a liar,

Leah was ugly,
Joseph was abused,
Moses had a stuttering problem,
Noah was a drunk,
Gideon was afraid,
Sampson had long hair and was a womanizer,
Rahab was a prostitute,
Jeremiah and Timothy were too young,
David had an affair and was a murderer,
Elijah was suicidal,
Isaiah preached with no clothes on,
Jonah ran from God,
Naomi was a widow,
Job went bankrupt,
John the Baptist ate bugs,
Peter denied Christ three times,
The disciples fell asleep while Jesus was praying,
Martha worried about everything,
The Samaritan woman was divorced more than once,
Zacchaeus was too small,
Paul was too religious,
Timothy had an ulcer,
and Lazarus was a dead man!

Somehow, despite their shortcomings, God used them to accomplish His purposes.

Some musicians are so skilled at what they do that they can make a bad instrument sound good. Sometimes we see a coach put somebody we think is terrible in the game, and yet the person ends up helping to win the game. Then we say, "I guess the coach knew what he was doing." God is sort of like that. He can take little old imperfect us and use us to make a beautiful creation. So if you sense that God wants to put you in the game and use you in some way, don't worry about your shortcomings. Just believe that God knows what He's doing.

Hmm …

—Did anybody ever ask you to do something that you felt ill-equipped to do? How did you handle it?

—Did you ever feel that God was moving you to do something that you felt ill-equipped to do?

—Why do you think God chose Moses to do the task he needed done instead of somebody with more clout and more speaking ability?

—When you look at the list of all the famous biblical names and realize how flawed they were, what do you think?

—What do you think God teaches us about Himself by using the people he did?

## chapter twenty-two

# Never Up, Never In

On the golf course, my name is Alice. I know this because my playing partners so often say to me, "Come on, hit it, Alice." You have to understand that my playing partners are usually older men who have the old-fashioned view that women are the weaker sex. They therefore consider it an insult to call a fine specimen of a man such as myself by a woman's name, just because I didn't hit the ball hard enough.

If you don't play golf, you need to understand that golf is a game invented by people who lived in old Scotland. These are the same people who first thought that music comes out of a bagpipe. Therefore, you know that their judgment was poor.

I don't play golf very much; therefore, I'm not very good at it. But there is a lot of social pressure to keep some of my friends company once in a while as they go out and pretend to have fun using a skinny stick to hit a little ball into a little hole that is four hundred yards away. It seems to me that the most fun they have is teasing me.

Another thing they say to me a lot is, "Never up, never in." Old people repeat themselves frequently. So when I'm on the green, which is that short grass nearest the hole, and I'm trying to roll the ball those last few yards into the hole, if I don't hit it hard enough, they shake their heads and say, "Come on, hit it, Alice. Never up, never in." over and over. "Never up, never in" means that if you don't hit it hard enough, there is no way the ball will go in the hole, even if you hit it straight. So they say it is better to hit it too hard than too soft. But it's scary to hit it too hard because sometimes you can end up further away from the hole than when you started. Their philosophy is, "Go for it. If you miss, you miss, but at least you gave it a chance."

My mind was meandering the other day when the pastor was talking about courageously obeying what you think God is telling you to do, even if it seems really weird. It's similar to "Never up, never in." If you feel that you are getting an inspiration to do or say something, but you are uncertain about whether it's an inspiration, you might chicken out. In that case, you never even gave it a chance to be right on. You might be way off, but what's the worst that could happen?

Here's an example. You might be riding down the street in a car with your friend and talking. Suddenly, the words "chocolate chip cookies" pop into your head, and you have this strong urge to mention that to your friend. You could chicken out and think that it's just too weird. On the other hand, if you mentioned it, your friend might say, "You know, I've had my grandma in Des Moines on my mind a lot, thinking I need to go visit her. One thing I remember her for is that she always made the best chocolate chip cookies. I think you are telling me I need to get down there." I mean, it might be that "chocolate chip cookies" popped into your head because you just drove by a cookie factory and smelled cookies. Your friend might laugh and point that out to you. That might be embarrassing, but it's not the end of the world. The thing is, if you chicken out, you don't even give God's inspiration a chance. As my golfer buddies say, if you miss, you miss, but at least you gave it a chance.

There are a lot of things that you might feel "inspired" to do, like call somebody and say hello, or offer somebody a ride, or buy a certain book, and so forth. You might think, "Why did that dumb idea pop into my head?" You never know.

Never up, never in. Go for it. Hit it, Alice.

Hmm …

—Have you ever felt inspired to say or do something that seemed too weird to do?

—Have you ever followed through on such an inspiration and had somebody really benefit from it?

—Have you ever followed through on such an inspiration and been embarrassed by the response?

—Do you look for opportunities to act on a feeling or an idea?

chapter twenty=three

# Church Is Like a Football Team

I was watching a football game the other day on TV. Within about five minutes from the start of the game, I could just tell that my team was going to get beat; so my mind started meandering.

I was thinking the church is kind of like a football team: we all want to get to the same goal, we all want to help the team win, we all want to please the coach, we all bring different skills to the game, and a team victory depends upon everybody doing their part.

Then I got to thinking about that different skills part. I remembered playing football in high school. I was the quarterback on our high school football team, but it wasn't because I could throw the ball. I was a catcher in baseball, and even when throwing the football, my passes all looked like throws to second base: hard and low. My coach once said to me, "Woody, the receiver is not trying to put a tag on somebody;

get the ball up where he can catch it." No, I was the quarterback because I had a photographic memory, and I liked studying the playbook. Once during practice, a bunch of guys in the huddle were asking what they were supposed to do on the play that had been called, and I could tell pretty much every position what they were supposed to do. One of the coaches overheard this. In high school football, 90 percent of winning the game is just getting people to run the correct pattern, block the right person, and be in the right spot. So, because I could explain this to each position, I got the job.

In high school football, you are generally assigned a position based on your shape. The guy who is five feet tall and five feet wide is generally the center. Our center was immovable. He couldn't move forward because he couldn't run, but the other team also couldn't move him backward. So, I would get the ball from him, just turn around, and stay on his tail because I trusted that nobody would be getting around him. I would then give the ball to one of these little guys that could run like the wind, and if everybody did what they were supposed to do, we'd get closer to the goal. If not, we'd have to pass. Aaannd then we had an adventure.

The tall, skinny kids were the pass receivers. They were really the basketball team, and they did not like getting hit. Plus they didn't see anything wrong with dribbling the ball a few times before picking it up. Passing was not our team's strong point. The coach would usually say the game plan is that we're going to do what we do best: "Woody will turn around and give it to Jimmy, and Jimmy will run like the wind."

Anyway, as I was saying before meandering into yesteryear, the church is kind of like that. Different people bring different skills to the mission. You have your bubbly, outgoing people to be greeters; you have your people that love kids, and they teach Sunday School; you have your accountants, your contractors; you have people who love to sort and distribute donated goods; you have musicians and you have singers; you have people who love computers; and bakers, shakers, and candlestick makers. Or as the Bible says, "To one is given through the Spirit the expression of wisdom; to another the expression of knowledge according to the same Spirit; to another faith by the same Spirit; to another gifts of healing by the one Spirit. But one and the same Spirit produces all of these, distributing them individually to each person as he wishes" (1 Corinthians 12:8–9, 12). I think Paul was saying that you can't say a person is not a Christian because they don't have the gift of healing or speaking in tongues or prophesying. They might just have the gift of faith or of loving people.

For a football team to be successful, every position must do its job. If everybody who showed up to try out for the football team was a little guy who could run like the wind, who would do the blocking? Who would do the kicking? As Saint Paul said, "If the whole body were an eye, where would the hearing be?" (1 Corinthians 12:17). Every gift, or talent, is important, and every member of the church has an important gift to offer the mission of the church.

The most important thing for a church's success, though, is what my coach said when a reporter asked him what it would take for us to beat the team ranked fifth in the state. He said, "It's gonna take a lot of prayer, Ralph, a lot of prayer."

Hmm …

—What gifts do you have to offer the church?

—Is the church aware that you have those gifts?

—Do you think your church needs what you have to offer?

—Have you ever been on a team when somebody failed to complete their assignment? How did that affect the other team members?

## chapter twenty-four

# It's How You Play the Game

I think that God gave us the technology to do instant replays so that good Christians would not have to yell nasty things at referees. I'm a big football fan, and I love to watch my favorite teams play. Winning is what it's all about, though, and those referees can cost you the game sometimes.

Wait, did I just say that winning is what it's all about? It seems that way, these days. But there was an old saying, "It's not whether you win or lose, but how you play the game that counts." We don't hear that saying much anymore. Seems like there's been a lot of news lately about athletes using performance-enhancing drugs. There are asterisks next to more and more records. Once again, my mind started meandering, and I started wondering about the value of winning and what Jesus would say about it all.

We Christians talk about winning quite a bit. There's an old hymn about "Victory in Jesus." We talk about defeating the devil. Saint Paul talks about putting on the armor of God so that we can stand firm in the evil day. A lot of the Old Testament is about

Craig Wood

God helping the Israelites to trample their enemies. In fact, the whole concept of the Messiah held by the ancient Jews was that the Messiah would be a King that would lead them to victory.

Yet, even though some of His followers were saying He was the Messiah, Jesus turned out to be a surprise and said some puzzling things. In the days of Jesus, winners in the game of life were thought to be rich people. Well, it's not much different these days, I guess. But in those days, people assumed that if you were rich, you were righteous and therefore blessed by God. But Jesus said, "For it is easier for a camel to pass through the eye of a needle than for a rich person to enter the kingdom of God" (Luke 18:25). Well, *that* certainly caused a lot of head scratching.

The disciples were arguing among themselves one time about which of them was the greatest. Jesus said, "For the one who is least among all of you is the one who is the greatest" (Luke 9:48). To be a winner in the eyes of Jesus meant being a servant. He said, "For who is greater, the one seated at the table or the one who serves? Is it not the one who is seated at the table? Yet I come to you as one who serves" (Luke 22:27).

Then there was that crazy parable about the landowner who hired men standing around in the marketplace to work in his field. He hired a bunch first thing in the morning. Then hired another bunch around noon, and some at 3:00 p.m., and some about an hour before quitting time. Then, he paid them all *the same wage!* Go figure. As you might expect, the ones that worked all day were just a little upset. The point of the parable, Jesus said, is that "the last will be first and the first will be last" (Matthew 20:16). And that great philosopher Leo Durocher said, "Nice guys finish last."

(Okay, for you youngsters, Leo Durocher was not really a philosopher; he was a baseball coach who was more interested in winning than in being nice.)

Maybe there is something to that old saying "It's not whether you win or lose but how you play the game that counts." So what does that mean? Well, in sports, it means you play by the rules and don't cheat, you don't stomp on your opponent when they're down, you work hard to develop whatever skill you have, you give your best effort, you don't get lazy, you never give up, and you don't yell at the referees if they make a bad call.

I guess all of that applies to the game of life too.

Hmm ...

—Why might it be difficult for a rich man to enter Heaven?

—What are the rules to the game of life? Have you added any? What kinds of things would be "cheating"?

—What do you think Jesus meant when he said, "the last will be first"? In our world, who is "last" and who is "first"?

# chapter twenty-five

# The Miracle of Modern Medicine

One of the things that old people talk about on their coffee breaks turns out to be colonoscopies. I had my fifth one last week. At first when I had one, I was all hush-hush about it because I thought it was sort of taboo to talk about it. But just before I had my third one, I was talking to a few people in the break room telling them that I was going to be off work the next day, and one of them got nosy and asked why. I kind of whispered, "I'm having a colonoscopy." I heard back, "You what?" "Speak up, I didn't catch that." "What are you having?" So I spoke louder and said, "A colonoscopy. I'm having a colonoscopy. Okay?"

Then it was, "Is this your first one?" "Been there, done that." "What kind of stuff did they give you to drink?" "Don't get very far from the toilet tonight." And then all of us over fifty started comparing notes about our experiences with colonoscopies.

If you are under fifty, you probably don't know what I'm talking about unless your parents talked to you about theirs. But, as I discovered a while back, doctors recommend that if you are over fifty, you ought to have a colonoscopy once every few years to make sure you don't have any colon cancer. For you uninitiated, a colonoscopy is a minor surgical procedure where the doctor runs a TV camera through your colon, also known as the large intestine, to check and see if there are any suspicious-looking bumps. If there are, he snips them off. The procedure is painless. The preparation is miserable.

They make you drink some awful-tasting stuff, and a lot of it, so that you will have to spend an evening on the toilet cleaning out your colon. I told the doc that if he would let me eat some chili with beans, it would have the same effect. But he didn't buy it. Anyway, I had to spend an evening with really not a lot to do but sit on the toilet and read and think. So, naturally, my mind started meandering.

One of the things I thought about is that it is pretty amazing that they have tiny little TV cameras with which they can go looking around inside your body. Can you imagine what the people who lived at the time of Jesus would have thought about being able to see a picture of the inside of your body? Things that doctors do today, a lot of which we take for granted, would be miracles to those people. And perhaps they *are* miracles.

I was thinking about my mom, who at the age of fifty-five had a brain tumor removed and would have died had she been living two thousand years ago. But because of the miracle of modern medicine, she was able to live to see several grandchildren graduate from high school and college and see them get married before she passed away at the age of seventy-six. Can you imagine what somebody living at the time of Jesus would have said if you told them you could cut the top of somebody's skull off, remove a disease from the brain, replace the top of the skull, sew the skin up, and send the person home to live for another twenty years? They would think *you* had a brain problem.

We now live in a world where a man with both legs amputated above the knee was disqualified from running in a race because of having an unfair *advantage*! Of course, if you have seen the artificial "legs" they made for the guy, you'd understand. They are kind of springy. Still, it would take quite a bit of training and work to get used to running on those. I have enough trouble trying to run on my actual ones.

When John the Baptist sent his followers to Jesus to ask if Jesus was the Messiah, Jesus said to them, "Go and tell John what you hear and see: the blind regain their sight, the lame walk, lepers are cleansed, the deaf hear, the dead are raised, and the poor have the good news proclaimed to them" (Matthew 11:4–5). These words would have apparently meant to John that Jesus was the Messiah and that the kingdom of Heaven was being ushered in.

The ancient Jews believed that the Messiah would be a great warrior king who would lead Israel to defeat their enemies. John's followers could have gone back to John and said, "We don't think this is the guy. The Romans are gaining in strength, Jesus has no army other than a bunch of poor and sick people following him around, unfair taxes are still being collected, and the Pharisees still run the temple for only the rich." But the message that Jesus gave them to take to John was different.

If John sent followers from a distant planet today and asked, "How goes it on Earth? Is the kingdom developing as it should?"

What would we say? We could say, "There are terrorists all over the place, the world's economy is shot, and the ice caps are melting." But we could also say, to a greater extent than ever before in this world, "The blind regain their sight (laser surgery), the lame walk (and run races), lepers are cleansed (and cancer is cured), the deaf hear (cochlear implants), the dead are raised (stopped hearts are restarted every day), and the poor have the good news proclaimed to them."

Despite all of the bad news, maybe the universe is unfolding the way that God intends for it to unfold.

Hmm …

—Why would it be a sign that Jesus was the Messiah for the poor to have the good news proclaimed to them?

—What would you describe as a God-given miracle?

—Do you think that modern medicine is a miracle? If not, what words would you use?

# chapter twenty-six

## Storing Up Treasures

I think we can learn a lot by watching cats. For one thing, they really know how to sleep. We have two cats, and when they curl up and go to sleep together, they really look warm and cozy. Cats can also always look dignified, even during a disaster.

I was watching one of our cats the other day as she decided to make a leap. Cats like to get as high as they can, maybe so they can look you in the eye, so they are always looking for some new way to get up off the floor. I had just opened a new vaporizer to help us breathe easier during the cold season, and I left the empty box on the table. After plugging in the vaporizer, I went back to throw the box away, and there was the cat, eyeballing the box. So I watched to see what she would do. Suddenly she jumped right for the top of the box, and she and the box went tumbling from the table all the way to the floor.

The cat turned quickly to make sure the box was not chasing her, and then sat and calmly started licking her paw and giving herself a bath, as if to say, "I'm cool. This is not a problem."

Then, of course, my mind started meandering. I was thinking that the cat would have been successful if the box had not been empty. It needed a firm foundation. She was sort of like the foolish man who built his house upon the sand, and it all came crashing down.

Often we are like my cat in that we try to raise ourselves up on things that are empty. I am thinking of things like money, clothes, peers, cars, or storage bins full of grain. Okay, not many of us have storage bins full of grain, but you get the point. You can probably think of more things than I can. Sometimes, those things even keep us high for a time before they come crashing down. I always feel bad when I hear about somebody who borrowed more than they could afford in order to buy a big house and end up losing the house, as well as the money they invested in it.

Jesus told us that we should not "store up treasures on earth" because they can easily come crashing down, but we should store up treasures in Heaven (Matthew 6:19–21). A little later, Jesus asked, "Can any of you by worrying add a single moment to your life span?" (Matthew 6:27).

Sometimes, our earthly treasures never crash for real, but we worry about it anyway. We kind of know that the potential is always there that, in their emptiness, they will come crashing down. If they do come crashing down, we need to be able to lick our paws and give ourselves a bath and say, "I'm cool. This is not a problem. My real treasure is in Heaven."

So how do we do that if we're not a cat? I think that we have to accept the Word of Jesus that God loves us. Our value is not based on how many storage bins full of grain we have or how many cars or computers or sneakers we have. Our value is based on God's love for us.

We are so valuable that God allowed His Son to come to earth for our sakes, knowing that He would suffer in the desert, that He would be ridiculed by the priests, and that he would be tortured on the cross. That means we are pretty valuable. Think about it. Would you allow your kids to go help somebody if you knew that those kids would endure great suffering? You would really have to value the person needing your kids' help. So we have to know that we are very valuable in God's eyes. We have to know that, as somebody else once said, "God don't make no junk." But our value is not based on our possessions. Our value is, again, based on the fact that we are children of God, and He loves us.

Hmm …

—In the old days, people based their value on how many storage bins of grain they had. What do we base our value on today?

—The original Colonel Sanders of Kentucky Fried Chicken fame once said, "It does me no good to be the richest man in the cemetery." What are your thoughts on that?

—Are you standing on any empty boxes right now? What can you do if they start to wobble or even collapse?

# chapter twenty=seven

## Throwing Stones

When I was little, I would sometimes sit staring off into space daydreaming. Even back then my mind meandered. Anyway, if Mom were around, she would say, "A penny for your thoughts." And I would usually tell her my thoughts. I might be daydreaming about hitting a home run at the Little League game that night, or I might be thinking about taking the fender off my bike so it would look really cool. Or I might be plotting some way to get even with the kid down the block (or maybe I'd keep that one to myself). If I were a kid these days, I would probably say, "A penny!? Mom, you've got to be kidding! Make it a dollar, and maybe we can talk."

Actually, these days, no amount of money could get me to reveal some of my thoughts. I have looked at people and had thoughts about them and said to myself, "I am sure glad that person cannot read my mind right now."

For example, not long ago I walked by a man wearing shorts, and I thought to myself, "That guy's legs are really ugly. Some guys just should not wear shorts." We probably all know guys like that. Nevertheless, it was a nasty thought, and I was glad the guy could not read my mind.

Then my mind meandered over to thinking about Heaven. I think when we get to Heaven, we will know everybody else's thoughts, and they will know ours. The Bible definitely says that God knows our thoughts (Luke 16:15). And the Bible also says that we will become one with the Father (John 17:23). So, I figure that in Heaven, thoughts are all out in the open. That's pretty scary.

I don't know if, when I get to Heaven, I will stop having nasty thoughts, or if people will just be more accepting and forgiving. I mean, I know that God knows all about my nasty thoughts, but I feel comfort in His love and understanding. It's *people* that scare me!

And I'm just as bad about judging people as anybody else. I've noticed, though, that I generally get judgmental about other people when they commit sins that I don't commit. For example, I am really critical of people who double park. That's a sin that's easy for me to avoid. I don't like people honking at me, and I don't mind walking a couple of blocks, so I just go until I find a legitimate parking spot. But I didn't get critical at all during the sermon the other day when the pastor confessed to speeding. I, too, tend to drive a little over the speed limit from time to time; so I'm more forgiving on that one. But I never double park. So guess who makes me really angry: it's the people who double park. Speeders? Well, that's a live and let live kind of thing, right?

I'm starting to think that we really need to get over worrying about other people's sins. First John says, "If we say 'We are without sin' we deceive ourselves, and the truth is not in us. ... We make Him a liar, and His Word is not in us" (1 John 1:8, 10). So, I'm guessing that if we remember our own sins when we start to yell at somebody else for theirs, we wouldn't yell so much. Or, as Jesus said, we need to stop worrying about the splinter in somebody else's eye and get the two-by-four out of our own, or something like that (Luke 6:41).

We need to ask Jesus to remind us that only those who are without sin can throw stones at other people. I'm guessing that when we go to Heaven, we all will have to leave our bag of rocks at the door. And I must tell you, that's a relief to me because I have a hunch there are a bunch of people who could find fault with some of my behavior.

Hmm …

—What kinds of "sinners" make you the angriest?

—What kinds of things do you find easy to forgive in others?

—How can we learn to be more understanding and less judgmental of others and ourselves?

—What are your thoughts on the saying, "Hate the sin, but love the sinner"?

## chapter twenty-eight

# Graven Images

I hate to say it, but I am a worshiper of graven images. I love pictures. I love family photo albums and family videos. I take hours of video of stuff most people get bored watching, like my daughter painting her house. When we watch those videos, the family usually says, "Can we fast forward through this part?" But I love to take them and edit them and watch them, even if I just watch them all by myself.

Back in the old days, photographs were actually engravings. Even that term *graphics* has its roots in the word *engravings*. Grav, graph; see what I mean? Photographs probably qualify as graven images. These days, of course, photos are all digital. So maybe I'm off the hook. Let me check.

Nope. It definitely says right there in Exodus 20:4 (RSV), "You shall not make for yourself a graven image, or ANY likeness of anything that is in heaven above, or that is in the earth beneath, or that is in the water under the earth." I guess I get caught on that "any likeness" part. Of course it goes on to say, "You shall not bow down to them or serve them." So, some people might say it's okay to make likenesses of things so long as you don't worship them.

But I come pretty close to worshiping family pictures. I've often thought that if my house were burning down and I had to choose what to grab on the way out, I'd probably grab my family videos. How can you replace the family videos? I suppose if I were technologically savvy and I wanted to pay a subscription fee, I could store them all in that "cloud" people talk about. But I'm not and I don't, so my family videos are all on DVDs. Last winter I made a DVD of my dad from twenty years of the old VHS videotapes. I'm pretty sure that for a couple of months there I spent more time editing video than I did reading the Bible. Actually I spent more time editing video than I did on just about anything else. In fact, my wife was wondering if I'd *ever* shovel the walk.

Speaking of the Bible, that could also be considered a graven image. The art of using a printing press is called typography. There's that "graph" thing again. But I suppose if you don't worship the Bible as a god, some people would say it's okay to make that graven image called the Bible. They might also say it's okay to even own one. There was a time, back in the Middle Ages, when it was against the law to own a Bible. A person could get put in prison or even executed by the church for having one.

Fortunately, these days, it's okay to own one. In fact, some people, including our pastor, might say you *better* own one, and you better *read* it. But I've seen it happen where a person will make a god out of the Bible instead of using the Bible to see God.

It's kind of like confusing the TV set with the person who is seen speaking in it. There have been times when I felt like shaking the

TV because the person speaking in it was making me mad. But the TV is not the person. And the Bible is not God. God speaks to us through the Bible, just as people speak to us through a TV. It is important not to confuse the medium with the entity to which the medium connects us. Sometimes God doesn't use the Bible; sometimes God hits us with a bolt of lightning, as was done with Paul. If you think about it, God was speaking to people a long time before the Bible existed.

Some translations of the Bible use the word *idol* in place of *graven images*. Making an idol and worshiping it is called idolatry, and God does not want us worshiping anything but God. So, Moses got extremely mad when the Israelites made a golden calf and called it God. Then what about little crosses and fishes that represent Jesus? My view is that if we don't get the symbol confused with God, it's okay to have those reminders.

Actually, I think that what God wants us to do is just to not make God less than what God is. God has no boundaries and no limits, and to make something solid that we can try to put God into is making God what *we* want God to be instead of just experiencing what God is.

There was a time in ancient Judaism when it was prohibited to even utter God's name. They believed during that time that speaking God's name belittled Him. Giving something a name makes it a thing—a being with boundaries and limits. When Moses asked God how to refer to Him when he spoke to the Jews, God said to tell them that "I Am Who I Am" had sent him (Exodus 3:14). Some translators say it was stated as "I Am the One Who Is." My mind meandered to this thought: God is not *a* being but *is* Being. Paul Tillich put it this way: God is Being Itself. That seems pretty consistent with the concept as told to Moses. It seems that God did not want to be limited by having a name.

Hmm …

—Has God ever spoken to you other than through the Bible?

—Are there any other books that God "wrote"?

—How can we think of God without making God a being or giving God a name?

## chapter twenty-nine

# It All Pays the Same

We were heading to see the fireworks downtown this past Fourth of July just shortly before dark, which was close to 9:30 p.m. They were scheduled to begin at 9:45 p.m., and a large crowd had already gathered. Nevertheless, we were able to plop our folding chairs down in a place where we had a good view of the action.

Back when the city first started doing this, though, I would take the lawn chairs downtown about four hours ahead of time to make sure we got good seats. I would sit there in the heat getting sunburned saving seats for my wife and two children. There were a few other nuts like me arriving early and staking claim to the "good" spots. Most people, however, had the sense to wait until closer to the actual show. And then there were those who came at the last minute and squeezed in between me and the people behind me, making it a little crowded but not necessarily unbearable.

Nevertheless, it really irritated me that I had gone to the trouble of sitting in the heat all day to get a good view, and these clowns were going to see the same show and had probably been in air conditioned comfort all day. The nerve. For some reason, the show wasn't as enjoyable to me knowing that these other people hadn't "earned" the right to see it like I had. Anyway, I learned my lesson. After only two or three years of going early and getting sunburned, I decided I could see the show just as well even if I didn't go downtown early and suffer all afternoon. Pretty smart, eh?

As I thought about that recently, my mind started meandering, and once again I was reminded of the parable that Jesus told about the landowner who hired some workers in the morning for a wage that they were happy to receive. Then he kept hiring more workers and even hired some who only had to work the last hour before dark. As you might recall, he paid them all the same. I can just see the union putting up with that these days. Naturally, the guys that got hired in the morning complained.

Jesus said, "My friend, I am not cheating you. Did you not agree with me for the usual daily wage? Take what is yours and go. What if I wish to give this last one the same as you?" (Matthew 20:13–14). If I were saying that, I might put it this way: "What is your problem? You and I had a deal, and you were happy with our deal. Why are you worried about my deal with these other guys?" It's kind of like, I went to the fireworks show early to make sure I got a good view and to see a good show; and I achieved my mission—I saw a good show. Why should I be upset because somebody else got to see a good show?

My son was telling me not long ago about a conversation he had with a couple of his friends in the wee hours of the morning following a party. He was a college student at the time, and some of those late-night/early-morning conversations could get philosophical. They were talking about the pros and cons of Christianity. A couple of his friends were suggesting that if you can be saved at the last minute, as in a murderer who is born again just before being executed, then why should anybody be "good"? Why not just wait until the last minute? That way you can have fun your whole life, ask for forgiveness on your deathbed, and still go to Heaven. Of course, one of the problems with that logic is that you don't always die on a "deathbed." You might get hit by a truck and not have a chance to ask for forgiveness.

But there is also something about that logic that smacks of resentment of people that get saved at the last minute, that somehow because you made the decision earlier, you are more deserving of salvation. In our weekly discussion group, we are reading a book called *What's So Amazing About Grace?* One of the things I learned from that book is that the message of the parable of the workers is that *nobody* actually *deserves* salvation. It's a gift to *every*body.

And, of course, my son's friends had another problem with their logic. It is not true that you have to give up fun in order to be a Christian. Becoming a Christian is not exactly like sitting in the hot sun all day. I've been to some Christian parties, and I've been to some college kid parties. The only difference between them is that I can actually remember the fun I had at the Christian parties.

Hmm ...

—Does it bother you that some people are saved who have been saved on their deathbeds after having sinned their entire lives?

—How can you keep your focus on your own behavior and goals without worrying about what other people are doing?

—Do you think non-Christians have more fun than Christians?

—How would your life be different if you were not a Christian? Would you behave differently?

# chapter thirty

---

# Life Is a Jazz Gig

---

Let's get serious. The real question before us is whether life is a jazz gig or a symphony.

I am a jazz musician. Well, at least on weekends. Not many people can make a living playing jazz, so I do other things during the week to pay the rent. Anyway, I like to think life is like a jazz gig. Jazz is taking a composer's piece of music and adding your own little twist to it. You can't just play anything you want; you must stay within the basic structure of the song, or the result would be total disharmony with the other players in the band. So there is a sort of disciplined freedom involved in performing jazz music.

Classical musicians, on the other hand, play only the notes that are written by the original composer. Having been trained in classical music, as well, I can appreciate the result of a well-performed symphony. However, the art that has been created is mostly the art of the composer. To some extent, the conductor has an impact on the sound. But usually, the conductor and musicians try to stay true to what they believe was the composer's intent. And it does take a lot of talent to make the instruments sound the way that the composers of symphonies wanted it to sound. It is a little problematic that most of these composers died a couple hundred years before electricity; so there are no recordings of exactly how they thought it should sound.

The argument that life is a symphony goes like this: God has written the masterpiece, and it is our responsibility to play it the way He wrote it. The argument for jazz is that God wrote the music, but it is our responsibility to make something of it.

Saying that life is like a symphony is arguing in favor of predestination, or the notion that God has finished His creation, and the CD is playing out just as God intended, regardless of what we do. Arguing for the jazz side would be saying that, though God set up the basic structure, we have some choices to make about how the finished product ends up. That argument would say that we are kind of cocreators with God and are given the freedom to make some choices.

I think it is clear that we did not make a lot of the choices about who we are. We did not choose to be born in this time or in this country. We did not even choose our parents and how we were raised. All of that and more was "composed" for us, and it has a big impact on the music we create. The Bible says, "And those he predestined he also called; and those he called he also justified; and those he justified he also glorified" (Romans 8:30). So, there is some biblical support for the idea that it was all laid out for us. But earlier in that chapter, it says, "For creation awaits with eager expectation the revelation of the children of God," and "We know that all creation is groaning in labor pains even until now" (Romans 8:19, 22).

I said earlier that somebody once said that "what we are is God's gift to us; and what we become is our gift to God." So it seems to me that, although we were chosen and found and called, who we become—our creation—is a work in progress, something that is being born, and "creation awaits with eager expectation" what we will do with the piece of music handed to us.

The good news is that even if we make some bad choices that could cause us major problems, God helps us. One of the most graceful people in my life is the lady on the GPS in my car. When I make a wrong turn, she doesn't yell at me and say, "No! No! No! Turn around!" She calmly says, "Recalculating." Then she starts giving me directions as to how to get back on the right path to my destination. I think that's kind of how Jesus said that God works in us.

Hmm …

—If God sets the framework for our lives, what sorts of details become our choices?

—How do you make those choices for you? For example, do you study research on the topic, talk to people (if so, whom), or just think it over?

—Are U-turns allowed in life? Is there a reset button?

—Or do you think that life is a symphony, and we just need to play it the way it was composed to stay out of trouble?

# chapter thirty-one

# God Is a Drummer

God is a drummer. Not many people know that. Some day when this is a commonly accepted truth, you will be able to say that you were among the first to hear it. Some people think God is a piano player, but the word *piano* appears zero times in the Bible. It's the same thing with the guitar and bass. So it seems very clear to me that God is a drummer, because tambourines, which are handheld drums, and cymbals are mentioned in the Bible.

God creates the tempo of life. To everything there is a season—a rhythm—and we feel best when we step in time with the tempo God sets (just like it's best if the band keeps time with the drummer). You can't dance a waltz if the drummer is playing a samba. Or, put another way, you can't dance hip-hop to a country and western song. Well, it is possible, but it doesn't feel quite right, and it's hard to keep it up for long. In the same way, when God is drumming a certain beat, it is a struggle to keep dancing your same old dance.

At work, we once took a personality test to see how we behaved in certain circumstances. It measured how our personalities fit with certain types of environments and our preferred way of behaving in those environments. One of the things the instructor told us was that we could always do things that did not fit us—that were not our preferred way of behaving—but it just took more energy. So if you tested out as an extrovert, who are the ones who love to be around people, and if you had to sit alone and work at a computer all day, you would get very tired. On the other hand if you tested out as an introvert, and you had to go to meetings and talk to people all day, you would burn a lot of energy. It's like writing left-handed if you are right-handed. It can be done, but it takes a lot of effort. On the other hand, if you are engaged in activities that fit your personality, you tended to *gain* energy—become energized. So, if you are an introvert, you can be alone with a computer all day and not get tired, and if you are an extrovert, you can talk to people in meetings all day and not get tired. In the same manner, if your dance fits the beat and the music, you will feel better than if you try to waltz to a samba.

What is the rhythm of life? You wake up in the morning, go to work, go home at the end of the day, do your evening activities, go to sleep, and start the next day all over again. Of course, if you work third shift, then you start the song at a different place. The point is that life is kind of a song or a dance, and there is a rhythm to it. And the question is who is the Lord of your dance? To whose beat do you keep step? And how do you find the right "station" to even hear the beat?

Sometimes it seems like we say we want to live according to God's rhythm, but we really want to do our own dance instead of the dance He is playing. If that is the way it is for you, life might feel as if you're trying to write with the wrong hand. I know it certainly happens for me that way at times.

I was in a hurry to get somewhere the other day, and I hit every red light possible. I became quite agitated. Just when I thought it couldn't get any worse, I found myself behind somebody who would not make a left hand turn on a yellow light and sat through *three* red lights. I can tell you I was not feeling God's love for that person. Naturally, I arrived at the meeting late. As it turned out, several other people, including the main speaker, were late, and so it didn't matter anyway. I needed to just relax and accept God's tempo and play along with the song. I had burned a lot of energy being agitated instead of just going with the flow. And even if the meeting had started without me, it would not have been the end of the world.

And so I think that if we want to dance to the beat of a different drummer, there are times when we might have to do a different dance.

Hmm …

—Have you ever felt that there was a rhythm to life?

—When you are having a "bad day," and things aren't going quite right, how do you get through it?

—Try writing with your nondominant hand. How does that feel?

—There is a song in some hymnbooks called the "Lord of the Dance." Google it.

# chapter thirty-two

## The Right Stuff

The announcement came in a small envelope that looked on the outside to be an invitation. When we opened it, we read the shocking news: "God has blessed our family with an Immaculate Conception. Our daughter is to bear God's child. God said if it is a boy it shall be named Michael, and if it is a girl it shall be named Michelle. Praise God!"

Well, right away, one of the more cynical ladies in our group of friends said, "If God conceived that baby, He'd know whether it was a boy or a girl."

And that wasn't the half of it. I mean tongues were wagging among all who had heard the news. I'm surprised phone lines didn't melt. Okay, this happened before cell phones were invented. Anyway, I heard comments like:

"Do you suppose the girl made that story up, and why would the parents believe her?"

"Or if she didn't make it up, did the parents tell her to be quiet and *they* made it up?"

"Would you have the nerve to send something out like that even if you believed it?"

"I thought the Second Coming was on a horse out of the clouds.

It was pretty unbelievable.

Then the teenager miscarried, and the baby was not born after all. We never heard why the family thought God put them through all of that. The whole thing was never discussed much. Nobody wanted to embarrass the parents or the girl, who eventually had a normal life with a normal husband and normal kids. (Well, you know, as normal as anybody else anyway.)

My mind meandered over to that event the other day when I was thinking about Christmas and Mary and Joseph and how all of that came about. We don't really think much about it, or at least I don't, but can you imagine what Mary's parents must have thought when she came home one day and said to them, "God says I'm going to have His baby, and the baby is going to be the Messiah." This is a teenager who was betrothed, which in those days and the Jewish culture of that time was as good as being married except she still lived at home with her parents. So, you also must wonder about Joseph, her betrothed, who, of course, knew that if Mary was pregnant, he didn't do it.

In ancient Israel, if a betrothed teenager got pregnant by somebody other than her husband-to-be, she was to be stoned to death. Mary's parents are not mentioned in our Bible. There are some other ancient writings that talk about Mary's parents, but those writings did not make the cut when they were putting the Bible together. Those writings say that Mary's parents were Anne and Joachim. I don't know if that's true or not, but whoever they were, they were the right people for the job, because they did not stone Mary to death and stop the coming of the Messiah before it even got started.

We know Joseph was a righteous man, according to Matthew; and he could have insisted upon the law being followed. But he decided to divorce her quietly so as not to bring shame and the anger of the citizens upon Mary (Matthew 1:19). Some other zealot could have decided to take the law into his own hands and started stoning Mary. Then God spoke to Joseph, and Joseph did not even divorce Mary but maintained the image that things were fine so that tongues would not be wagging and stones would not be tossed (Matthew 1:20). God chose the right man to be Mary's husband.

It was probably good timing that Caesar Augustus called for people to go to their hometowns and register for a census right about the time that Mary would be getting really big. It gave Mary and Joseph an excuse to leave town and avoid a lot of questions. Then Jesus was born and lived during the Roman occupation of Israel so that eventually Rome would become a Christian nation and spread the gospel throughout Western civilization. And none of that would have happened if Mary's parents and Joseph had done what their law told them to do. They did what they heard God telling them to do.

The right people with the right stuff at the right time. I guess God knew what He was doing. Amazing!

Hmm ...

—Have you ever had a situation where you thought maybe God was telling you to do something other than what the Bible tells you?

—If you had been Mary's parents, could you have obeyed the law?

—Have you ever had somebody tell you that God gave him or her a message that was hard for you to believe?

Craig Wood

## chapter thirty=three

# Tough Questions

I have four grandchildren ages five to twelve. I love talking to them, finding out about their school life and their friends, what they like to do, and what their goals are. But sometimes they have some pretty tough questions. They ask things like:

"Why do you have to live in another town; why can't you just live in our house?"

"Why can't we just live at Disney World?"

"Why do you and Grandma have to have two cars?"

"How does that plane get up there?"

"Why doesn't your phone have any games on it?"

At their stage of development, some things are just incomprehensible, especially the one about my phone not having any games on it. I said they could go talk to their grandma about the two cars question. That's incomprehensible to me too.

At our stage of spiritual development, some other things are pretty incomprehensible as well. I have the feeling that Jesus got pretty frustrated at times trying to explain things to us in language that we would understand. God probably told Him to dumb it down for us, and I'm sure He tried His best. But one time, He said to a Pharisee, "You are a teacher of Israel and you don't understand this? If I tell you about earthly things and you do not believe, how will you believe if I tell you about heavenly things?" (John 3:10, 12).

Following a campout recently, during which she was bitten by several mosquitoes, my five-year-old granddaughter had this question: "Why did God even make mosquitoes? Doesn't God love us?" Try explaining to a five-year-old that because somebody who lived thousands of years ago broke God's rules, they got kicked out of the Garden of Eden, and now we all must suffer. That doesn't seem fair to her. Frankly, it doesn't seem fair to me.

I'm sure most of us have asked the question "Why do bad things happen to good people?" Or maybe even just "Why do bad things happen?" Some things are just incomprehensible to us. I have heard the question asked by people who don't call themselves Christian: "How can you justify the Catholic persecution of Protestants to the point of hangings?" (which happened in the sixteenth century). And some also ask, "How can you justify the Protestant persecution of Catholics to the point of hangings?" (which happened in the next century). Christians have not always come across to non-Christians as loving, caring, and forgiving individuals. Many of those in the Ku Klux Klan who killed black people were faithful members of Christian churches. Our non-Christian friends ask, "Are these things that God wanted to happen? If not, why does He allow it?" These things are incomprehensible to me and difficult to answer. But that does not mean that God is not real.

Craig Wood

There are other things that we find incomprehensible but still believe in. Here's one: my wife loves me. We have several areas of incompatibility. She is a vegetarian, and I am carnivorous. She loves shopping, and I can't stand shopping (God sent Amazon to me.) And so on. Nevertheless, she loves me. It is incomprehensible, but it does not mean it's not real.

I suppose some folks will say it's a cop-out, but I just have to figure that things that we now find incomprehensible God will answer at some point, just as there are answers to our childhood questions—answers that we learn as we grow and develop. Maybe you have already figured it out. Observing how human beings have often twisted the Christian message, I think it is indeed a miracle that the good news that Jesus brought us about God's love for us and his forgiveness of us has survived.

Recently someone offered to pray for a family member's recovery from a serious accident. I was shocked when I heard her pray, "Please heal him as much as possible and help his family and friends accept him as he is." My first thought was if God can heal him a little, why not a lot? My mind meandered some around the idea of less than perfect healing and why that would be an outcome of prayer.

I have a friend whose twenty-five year-old son was diagnosed with leukemia and was really getting sick with it. A bunch of us met at church for a prayer meeting to pray for this dad and his son. I was having an internal struggle with why this was happening to this family of dedicated Christians, as if Christians shouldn't suffer. I was praying at one point and complained to God (not out loud), "God, a father really shouldn't have to watch his son die." I thought I heard God say, "I know what you mean, Craig. I had that happen to me one time."

Hmm ...

—How do you respond when your non-Christian friends challenge you with tough questions?

—What do you find to be the most successful response to these tough questions?

—What is the most challenging question for you to answer?

—Is God all-powerful? Do our choices limit His help in some way?

# chapter thirty four

# More on Unanswerable Questions

As you have already discovered, I do not know it all. There are still things that puzzle me—questions to which I do not have the answer.

Here are some more questions to which I have no answer:

—Why are there some guys who never haul anything but drive pickups? I had a friend in school who bought a brand new pickup. He was in medical school, and his dad had some money. He never hauled anything in that pickup except girlfriends, and they sat up front, so he didn't need the pickup. He could have hauled the girls around in a Volkswagen, or, with his money, a Chevy Corvette. I asked him why he bought a pickup, and he said he thought they were "cool." Judging by the beautiful girls he hauled around, he must have been right.

—Why do men always have to put the toilet seat down? Why can't women learn to put it back up when they're done? One would think that after fifty years of being married, I would stop asking this question. But I can't let it go.

—Why is gas always ten cents a gallon higher in the town in which I live than in any other town in the state? I think where I live is even closer to the pipeline transfer where they load the trucks; so it ought to be cheaper here. I don't understand. And every station in town has the same price even though they, of course, do not engage in illegal price-fixing. They must just read each other's minds.

—How can the great-grandson of a monarch butterfly find the same *tree* in Mexico that his great-grandfather wintered in the previous winter? This is one of those mysteries that even scientists cannot solve. I mean the young butterfly is twice removed from the original visitor, yet somehow goes to the exact same place. What do they do, take photos and implant them on the genetic code somehow?

—Oh. And speaking of things I don't know, a friend who is age five pointed out to me the other day that I don't know the difference between a scratch and an ow-ie. She asked me about a small circular scab I had on my arm, and I said, "Oh, that's just a scratch." She said, "That's not a scratch, silly; that's an ow-ie. A scratch is a long skinny thing." Well. Live and learn. Now I know.

Sometimes I have questions about things I read in the Bible. The other day I was reading in the book of Matthew about the betrayal of Jesus. I found myself feeling sorry for Judas, the betrayer. The poor guy felt awful when he saw what was happening to Jesus.

He ended up throwing the blood money back to the chief priests and killing himself. My mind started meandering.

When Judas betrayed Jesus, was he doing God's will? And if he was, was he being good or evil? Did he go to Heaven or Hell? I had found more questions to which I do not have the answer.

God's plan of salvation seems to have been in place almost since the Original Sin. There are many hints in the Old Testament that things would happen as they did. Jesus Himself said that things had to go a certain way in order for the scriptures to be fulfilled. Jesus had to be the sacrificial lamb and die on the cross in order for us to be saved. So I was thinking that maybe Judas was just doing what had to be done in order for us to be saved.

If Judas had not betrayed Jesus, He would not have been arrested and hung on the cross, and we would not be saved. So we really ought to thank Judas for his part in our salvation. Right?

I brought this question up in our discussion group one time. One of the more astute members of our group pointed out that in Luke's version of the story, Satan entered Judas and prompted the deal with the chief priests to betray Jesus for thirty pieces of silver. She found it difficult to reconcile Satan having a role in the betrayal with the notion that God's will was being done. Another member pointed out that maybe God did not really want the betrayal and hanging of Jesus, but just knew that, people being what they were, it would happen that way. In other words, God could count on the evil nature of people to help His plan succeed. Then another member said, "You know what? I don't know why a computer works either, but I know it works." Well. Live and learn. See? This is one good reason to get involved in a discussion group: you can bounce ideas off people and learn stuff. Another good reason is that somebody always brings some good dessert to eat.

Anyway, maybe that's the answer. I need to stop worrying about whether Judas was good or evil and work on God's plan for me. In the parable of the workers who started at different times but got the same wage, Jesus said each of us is to be concerned with God's deal with *us* and not be concerned about God's deal with somebody else. In other words, I need to worry less about whether Judas was doing God's will and more about whether I, as in *me, myself, and I,* am doing God's will.

Hmm …

—Did Jesus have to die on the cross for us to be saved? Why do you think that?

—How do you know if you are doing God's will?

—Can doing something bad eventually lead you closer to God and His forgiveness?

Craig Wood

*chapter thirty-five*

# What Is God Thinking?

Sometimes you just gotta wonder what God's thinkin'. When bad things happen to good people, it's hard to figure.

The author of the book of Job was wondering about that. People living in those days believed that if you were a moral, upstanding, righteous citizen, you would have good crops, many sons (to help with the crops), and a long life. If you were bad, then you were barren, in crop production as well as in having children. You couldn't produce fruit of any kind.

But some observers began to keep score, and they figured out that it seemed to rain on the just and the unjust. They noticed that sometimes the righteous suffered and sometimes the bad guys did pretty well. The writer of Job struggled with this question of why God would cause a model citizen to suffer the worst of the worst.

Job's "friends" kept coming to him and saying, "You know what? You *must* have done something to anger God. Just confess it." Job said, "Far be it from me to account you right; till I die, I will not renounce my innocence" (Job 27:5).

In the end, we learn that God is painting a bigger picture than we can imagine. Our puny little minds cannot begin to grasp how it is all going to fit together. So wondering what God is thinking is not usually very satisfying because we're not up to it.

Harold Kushner wrote a book called *When Bad Things Happen to Good People*, a modern version of the Job discussion, after he had struggled with the death of his little boy. One of the things he says near the beginning is that if we try to answer the question about why bad things happen to good people, we need to first define "bad things" and then "good people."

The forbidden fruit on the tree in the Garden of Eden was on the Tree of the Knowledge of Good and Evil. It was described as the temptation to become God. And trying to be God by eating of the Tree of the Knowledge of Good and Evil is what got Adam and Eve into trouble. Maybe trying to figure out what are "bad things" and who are "good people" is not such a good idea.

Somebody once called Jesus good, and He got mad. He said, "Why do you call me good? No one is good but God alone" (Luke 18:19).

But Jesus is our spotless, sacrificial lamb. If anybody could claim to have suffered unjustly, it was Jesus. And his disciples must have been wondering what God was thinking by allowing Jesus to die. In their minds, the Messiah was supposed to be a conquering hero, a mighty king. If you had been standing there watching the Roman soldiers taunt and torture Jesus on the cross, would you have even begun to think that someday the Romans would be responsible for spreading the gospel throughout the Western world? Jesus did eventually conquer Rome, just not in the way those early disciples thought he would.

God was painting a bigger picture than they could imagine. And their sadness turned into our joy. And our faith is that even though it doesn't always make sense to us, somehow in the end it will be okay.

Hmm ...

—Have you ever felt that God was unjustly punishing you or somebody you know?

—Imagine yourself at the foot of the cross. What would you be thinking?

# chapter thirty-six

## God's Gift Card

Some people think that we have overcommercialized Christmas. That might be true. But I sometimes think about the fact that if Jesus had not been born, a lot of stores would go broke. A lot of stores lose money all year but make enough money selling Christmas presents to carry them through. We should just walk into those stores and tell them: "You are only making a profit because Jesus was born." Well, maybe we shouldn't really. If they are Christians, they already know that, and if they're not, we'd just make them mad.

Speaking of commercials, I think it would be fun to be one of those people that write funny TV commercials. Maybe we could do some for Jesus. Instead of the Aflac duck, we could have an owl. You could have a scene where a couple were arguing about how to make ends meet, and their neighbor steps in and says, "You know who could help this situation?" and the owl would go "Who?" Then the word *Jesus* would flash on the screen. Or maybe we could get a little green lizard with an Australian accent to say something like, "Come with me, mate, and we could save lots of blokes!"

Obviously my mind has been meandering about Christmas recently. I am taking some comfort in the fact that the spirit of Christmas giving is symbolized by a chubby old man with flowing white hair. I mean if you watch today's movies and TV shows, most of the heroes are, like, twelve. At best they are not over twenty. So for the hero of this important annual event to be a senior citizen makes me feel that I still have something to offer.

Of course the real hero of Christmas is God, not Santa Claus. Some people picture God as an old man with flowing white hair. Maybe they got Him mixed up with Charlton Heston, who played Moses in the movie. And maybe I'm the only one old enough to remember that movie. Anyway, God has been around awhile; so maybe He is the definitive Senior Citizen. I don't think He looks like Santa Claus or Charlton Heston, though. I have a hunch that God does not age as we humans do. Whatever God looks like, it is hard to beat His Christmas gift. He changed the world with His love.

The gifts I give are pathetic. I buy clothes that people never wear. Last year I bought a "Infotainment System" to install in my wife's car, but before we could install it, the car died, and we had to get a new car. Anybody need a car stereo for a '92 VW? Probably not. These days you just plug in your phone and play iTunes. Anyway, I spend all day on December 24 shopping and end up getting terrible presents for people. I don't understand it. Why are the stores all sold out of the good presents when I go shopping? Next year I'm going to get smart and go shopping on December 23. Or maybe I will just buy gift cards and tell people to get what they want. But some people think that's the lazy way out.

The more I think about it though, what God gave us was more like a gift card. Jesus is kind of a "one size fits all" gift. I figure we all got lost in a different place, but Jesus can find us and take us back to God no matter where we try to hide. What we need is what we get. We can take that gift, and we can apply it to our lives wherever we are on our journey.

What a gift!

I leave you with this excerpt from a poem by James Russell Lowell, called "The Vision of Sir Launfal":
Earth gets its price for what Earth gives us;
The beggar is taxed for a corner to die in,
The priest hath his fee who comes and shrives us,
We bargain for the graves we lie in;
At the devil's booth are all things sold,
Each ounce of dross costs its ounce of gold;
For a cap and bells our lives we pay,
Bubbles we buy with a whole soul's tasking.
'Tis heaven alone that is given away,
'Tis only God may be had for the asking.

Printed in the United States
By Bookmasters